Raise Your Voice 2

The Advanced Manual

Jaime Vendera

Vendera Publishing

Interior Design: Daniel Middleton
www.scribefreelance.com

Cover Design: Molly Burnside
www.crosssidedesigns.com

Editor: Richard Dalglish

Photography: Impressive Studios/Kevin Hoops
Photo Detail: Lonnie Winters/Jaime Vendera
Illustrations: Benoit Guerville

Audio Files: Recorded by Jaime Vendera and mixed by Austin Jenkins

ISBN: 978-1-936307-29-6

Printed in the United States of America

OTHER BOOKS BY JAIME VENDERA

The Official Guide to Jim Gillette's Vocal Power
Online Teaching Secrets Revealed
The Ultimate Vocal Workout Diary
The Ultimate Breathing Workout
Unleash Your Creative Mindset
Sing Out Loud books I-IV
The Air & Water Diet
Brand the New You
Reclaim Your Voice
Raise Your Voice
11 Simple Steps
What's Missing?
Vocal RESET
SpeakEasy
PractiSING
Voice RX
Singfit

I dedicate this book
To my friends, fans, and students
You're the fuel that drives me to do what I do

ATTENTION *Raise Your Voice 2* Owners!

This book comes with lifetime free access to the Raise Your Voice 2 Member's Section. The Member's Section contains all of the audio examples for this book to guide you through the Raise Your Voice 2 system.

To access the RYV2 Members Section, go to:

www.jaimevendera.com

From the homepage, click the Members link, and then click the RYV/RYV2 button. Enter your password from *Raise Your Voice.*
Next, click the "Raise Your Voice 2" link.
The password is:
"vocalmachine"

Note: All words that are **underlined bold** in this book refer to the audio files, which you can download from the Member's Section. Check out the first **Welcome** audio before reading on.

Contents

Introduction

ONE EXERCISE, ONE MINUTE, one new voice—that's no lie! Well, maybe I'm fibbing just a bit. Still, this amazing vocal exercise, which takes approximately one minute to perform (per each pitch), has the ability to build vocal muscle like never before! If you've been searching for an exciting new way to maximize your vocal potential, you've found the source.

Allow me to reintroduce myself. I'm glass-shattering vocal coach Jaime Vendera. I prefer to be called a voice-strengthening specialist, like one of my mentors, Elizabeth Sabine, has been called for years. I'm the guy that touring and recording artists contact when they can't hit the notes, when they've lost their voice and they need to sing that night, and when they're in fear of permanent vocal damage. What I teach them is what you'll learn in this book, because vocal strengthening is the basis of a strong, healthy voice.

Before you begin reading, you should know that this book is meant for the eyes of advanced *Raise Your Voice* users only, which is why you can only access the *RYV2* audio files by owning *RYV1*. It's my safety precaution to make sure you know the basics. If you haven't studied the techniques in *Raise Your Voice*, you're not ready for this book. Why? Think of it like this: If the Isolation exercises from *Raise Your Voice* are comparable to jogging, the new Isolation exercise from this book would be comparable to running a race in the Olympics!

If you're unfamiliar with my work, stop reading now. Go to venderapublishing.com to buy *Raise Your Voice*. Read and study the book thoroughly before attempting the tactics in this book. If you're already familiar with my methods and are a dedicated Isolation practitioner, read on ...

Some may be wondering why I didn't simply revise and release a new edition of *Raise Your Voice*. Truth be told, it would have been too overwhelming. What you'll discover in *Raise Your Voice 2* are new teaching tips and tactics I've developed after many years of training singers. The *RYV2* approach streamlines the Isolation exercises to work the voice harder and more efficiently, and it shortens practice time.

Why shorten practice time? Honestly, it was for my own selfish reasons. My schedule is swamped with recording, filming television shows, writing books, and creating new products for Vendera Publishing, as well as co-producing fiction books for 711 Press, not to mention teaching and running VenderaVocalAcademy.com. It left me little time for my own vocal needs. There were days when I failed to perform my exercises, and those days were occurring more frequently.

Realizing that I wasn't practicing what I preached, I continued experimenting with my Isolation exercises to create an Isolation exercise combination from warming up and working out the voice, which would consist of all three of my Isolation exercises and my three favorite warm-ups. Through trial and error, I finally designed one simple, easy-to-perform exercise, which I call the "Ultimate Isolation Exercise."

This new exercise was based on a process I've since dubbed *exercise stacking,* which is a method of combining, or "stacking," exercises to create deeper muscle burn by overworking the muscular coordination required for any given pitch.

The Ultimate Isolation Exercise stack consists of Lip Bubbles, Resonant Hums, and Gargling Tone to warm up the voice before digging into the real muscle work with Falsetto Slides, Transcending Tones, and Sirens, resulting in a six-exercise stack applied to any given pitch before moving up or down to the next pitch.

"Does this mean that we're finished with *Raise Your Voice,* Jaime?" Not by a long shot. Using this new exercise stack doesn't mean you can throw away all of the other exercises you learned in *Raise Your Voice.* I still do individual Sirens, Falsetto Slides, and Transcending Tones when teaching, as well as warm up to the *Beyond The Ultimate Vocal Warm Up* training video, *The Ultimate Vocal Warm Up, Rock & Metal Singer's Warm Up Routine,* and *Voice RX Warm Up* mp3s, even programmed scales from my TUNED XD app for revving up my own voice every morning or before a show. And I still slip in *Extreme Scream* exercises from screaminglessons.com, and *Jim Gillette's Vocal Power* scales as well as the advanced *Vocal Power* scales I've created for my students. And I still occasionally perform the *Ultimate Breathing Workout.*

I know it sounds crazy to have so many exercise options, but as a vocal coach I must continue to use the programs I've created as often as I can in order to stay at the top of my game for my students, both beginner and professional alike. And it's nice to change up your vocal routine once in awhile so that you don't grow bored. However, the Ultimate Isolation Exercise is my main voice-building tool, because I find that it allows me to stay vocally in shape with minimal practice time. It's the perfect exercise for the singer who has developed their voice, mastered their technique, but lacks the time for practice because of their job, radio interviews, etc., but still needs to stay at the top of their game.

Although you might be getting the impression that this exercise could be the lazy singer's quick solution, it should be noted that it is not; it is an advanced tool for warming up and working out the voice quickly and effectively without sacrificing quality, and it can only be performed by singers who have developed a bare minimum of two octaves.

With that said, this exercise won't be difficult to learn. In fact, if you understand my approach, you know there's nothing overwhelming about my vocal exercises (though they work you like a beast.) It's the same for the Ultimate Isolation Exercise; it's easy to learn ... but it's a beast to master.

To master the Ultimate Isolation Exercise, you must focus on breathing, support, and vocal placement while maintaining a clean, resonant tone on all five vowels. True mastery of this exercise will be based on your knowledge of vocal technique in combination with understanding my Isolation exercises.

Once it all falls into place, you'll be able to perform this advanced exercise in your sleep. Your voice will feel amazing, and your vocal strength and range will increase, all with less practice time. That doesn't mean you get to be lazy. It means you have to be more experienced so that every minute practiced is a quality minute. Just so we're clear, I'd never teach this exercise to a beginner, just as I'd never teach a beginner the advanced scales I created based on *Jim Gillette's Vocal Power* scales.

With all my jabbering about the Ultimate Isolation Exercise, you may be thinking that *RYV2* is going to be a long-winded book for the sake of covering one simple exercise. Not true. This book consists of seven chapters, each dedicated to revisiting the main points of *Raise Your Voice*. This time around, I'll be offering you nuggets of knowledge from my training philosophy vault. In my usual style, I'll make it fun, introduce you to some new vocal products, and add guest articles written by some of my close friends. We'll add new stretches to the Vocal Stress Release program and learn how to apply exercise stacking not only to the voice but also to the entire body as well. You'll also discover how to "stair-step" pitches to strengthen and expand your range and unlock tones within your voice that you never knew existed. Without further ado, let's revisit vocal technique.

DISCLAIMER: The following sections are not intended to prescribe, treat, prevent, or diagnose any illness. Consult your physician before attempting any of the following exercises or testing any listed products, vitamins, minerals, or herbs.

REVISITING VOCAL TECHNIQUE

THIS CHAPTER IS A QUICK TECHNIQUE refresher, plain and simple. Vocal technique is the key to a rock-solid voice. The *RYV* techniques have kept me and others in top vocal shape for years. In fact, during the filming of *Superhuman Showdown* for Maverick Television (Discovery Channel), a group of ENTs from Ohio State University examining my vocal cords were baffled by my ability to break glass with my voice and wail at over 120 decibels without showing signs of vocal fatigue or wear and tear on my vocal cords.

They were even more baffled at the size of the muscles surrounding my larynx. One doctor had said that the size of the muscles surrounding my vocal cords was comparable to the chest of a professional body builder. He suggested that my healthy voice and large vocal muscles were due to my vocal exercises. He added that my ability to scream for hours on end without losing my voice must be the result of my vocal technique. Bottom line, correct technique and vocal strength training is crucial to a singer's survival.

Don't skip this chapter! Although it will, for the most part, sound familiar, there are some new, innovative concepts to help you live and breathe your vocal technique. If you don't live and breathe your vocal technique, you're aiming for possible vocal loss and a short-lived career. With that said, let's dive into my three-step-technique approach.

STEP ONE: BREATHING

Breathe with the belly; 'nuff said. You should recall from *Raise Your Voice* that inhaling should be viewed as if you are filling the lungs like filling a vase with water from the bottom up. This will help to expand the belly, back, and ribs as you inhale. To clarify, you can expand the chest, but it should always expand last. You'll notice that when I break glass I tend to expand and lift the upper chest. I do this to utilize as much breath capacity as possible for long, loud screams. When singing, you typically won't need this much breath, so the chest, in most cases, will not need to fully expand.

You may wonder why the belly must expand until we look like the "before" picture on a weight-loss commercial. It's to allow freedom in the lungs for our maximum breath potential. If the stomach stays flat or caves in, or if the chest expands first and the shoulders rise, you've limited your fuel supply. Loosely translated, your fuel delivery system won't function at maximum efficiency. No need for further explanation, as you have *Raise Your Voice* and *The Ultimate Breathing Workout* to guide you through the breathing process. So let's move on to support.

STEP TWO: SUPPORT

Support is your gas pedal. Need higher notes, more volume, or some wicked grit? Just add more gas. Many might say my approach to breath support is "brute force." I assure you, they are seriously mistaken. If this were true, I'd have permanent vocal damage by now. My approach to breath support actually prevents vocal damage by minimizing the amount of breath released, thus minimizing vocal strain.

How is this possible? It's simple. By bearing down, you will tighten the stomach muscles without forcing excess pressure up against the diaphragm. The diaphragm can remain contracted longer, slowly returning to its natural position without excess force. The slow return minimizes the breath flow required to vibrate the vocal cords. Minimal breath saves the voice.

Some methodologies believe that support occurs best by sucking in the stomach or pushing the stomach out. Testing both the in and out approaches only caused me to experience excess breath release and vocal strain. It was even worse when I didn't use any support at all.

When I break glass with my voice or make the baby cry noise (as explained in *Raise Your Voice* and *Sing Out Loud*), it takes serious breath control, not serious breath release. Breaking glass does take tons of air, but it's a consistent stream as opposed to releasing a huge burst all at once. I love breaking glasses, but those little bastages can take up to thirty seconds or longer to break. Since I need all the fuel I can get for those long screams, I push down for support to minimize my fuel release and to protect my voice.

As I said, when you push down (like passing gas) you create an opposing tension between the diaphragm muscles and the abdominal muscles. Instead of the diaphragm muscle relaxing, it attempts to stay contracted against the abdominal muscles. Thus, less breath is released. I've never felt the same support and minimal breath release when sucking in or pushing out my stomach. The in or out approach (as well as no stomach tension at all) allows air to come barreling out of me, causing my voice to break.

Therefore, in my opinion, my approach to support is best. If you agree, it's safe to say that you're going to need strong abdominals for this type of support. Speaking of which, here's an exercise to strengthen your abdominal muscles. For those of you who've spent many a night on your back with *Raise Your Voice* on your belly, inhaling and exhaling, it's time to flip the body over. So flop over on all fours, grab *Raise Your Voice, The Ultimate Breathing Workout,* and this book and stack them on the floor. Lie down on your stomach with your belly on your stack of books. Rest your knees on the floor as a pivot point, or you can lock your legs and use your toes. Extend your hands straight out like Superman. As you inhale, use your stomach to raise your body off the ground. Next, exhale slowly and with control so that you are lowered at a slow, steady pace as you release your breath supply.

Inhale   Exhale

This breathing exercise works the back, intercostal, and stomach muscles, creating a solid core for singing! Practice time should last no more than five to ten minutes every other day. Now, on to placement.

STEP THREE: PLACEMENT

No matter whether you're speaking, singing, or barking, you must always feel the buzz in the roof of your mouth. The buzz lets you know that your vocal tone is unobstructed from excess tension in the neck and pharynx. You should always feel the buzz when singing, and you'll notice that you can feel the buzzing sensation from the very front of the hard palate (even on your upper teeth) to the very back of the throat at the cold spot (inhale quickly and you'll feel the cold spot) as you sing different vowels. I've discovered that by moving the buzzing sensation around on the roof of your mouth, you can maintain each specific vowel from the bottom of your range to the top. In *Raise Your Voice,* I discuss vowel modification, which is still useful. However, by moving the focus of the buzzing sensation to different palate positions, you can bypass vowel modification to maintain the vowel even on your highest notes.

The best focal point for palate buzz on each specific vowel is as follows:

1. Focus on the buzzing sensation coming straight up out of the throat into the soft palate on the vowels "A" as in "Play" and "Ah" as in "Father."

2. Allow the buzzing sensation to move forward onto the hard palate ridge where you place the tip of your tongue when you make the "L" and "T" consonants for the "E" vowel as in "Sweet" and "Oo" vowel as in "Food." Focusing the buzz forward will also make the top teeth buzz.

3. On the "Oh" vowel, as in "Toe," you should feel the buzz covering the entire palate from front to back, including the back of the top teeth, the hard palate ridge, the soft palate, and the cold spot.

INTRODUCING THE TEEPEE

Now for some advanced-technique tactics. Generally, the palate should maintain a dome shape when singing to give the buzz a home. The dome is created by a slight yawn on the micro-breath. On higher notes, I've found that the sides of the dome begin to cave in and down to create a teepee (or A-framed roof) shape in the roof of the mouth. The teepee helps focus those higher notes along a narrow line of the palate from the back of the palate to the front, for a strong, resonant tone. To experience the teepee, imitate your best Sean Connery or **Dr. Evil voice** to feel the dome changing shape. Regardless of the shape of the palate, as long as you feel the buzz it's a sign that your voice is free of unnecessary constriction. I always tell my students, "As long as you catch the buzz, you're good to go." I know what you're thinking—STOP IT! I want the teepee concept to become second nature for all my *RYV* singers, as this will help to maintain one fluid, flawless instrument from bottom to top. Start paying attention and think "teepee," "Sean Connery," or "Dr. Evil" on those higher notes as you sing and practice, and you'll notice a huge difference in your ability to sing higher without strain.

Before moving on, I want to address two simple points that will affect your approach to your vocal workout. Those points are the "A" vowel and the "relaxed throat."

First, I've always used the "A" vowel as in "Play" as opposed to using "Eh" as in "Sweat," which many coaches prefer. It is true that "A" is a diphthong (two vowels together) consisting of "Ah+Ee," but I hang onto the vowel sound somewhere between the "Ah+Ee," keeping my mouth in a slight smile position. As long as you don't close your mouth down to form an "E" at the end of the "A," you'll maintain the sound. I've used "A" for years because it was how I was trained, and I've never looked back.

Second, the "relaxed throat" technique philosophy is somewhat confusing. It does require tension in the throat to create sound, plain and simple. So how could the throat be relaxed? Let me explain. The internal muscles around the vocal cords tense to stretch and adduct the cords. Therefore there IS tension in the throat when singing. However, when vocal coaches say, "Sing with a relaxed throat," I believe they actually mean, "Sing without excess tension."

Excess tension is evident when you see the veins in someone's neck pulsating as they go for the money note. Neck tension is a subconscious way to help create pitch. It will only over-tighten the vocal cords, building up the breath supply below the vocal cords, as well as cause the pharynx to squeeze in upon itself. Both actions will inhibit the release of pure vocal tone. This unnecessary pressure is like stepping on a water hose and holding back the pressure. The pressure will build up and eventually burst the hose.

If you're straining when singing, you're obviously creating excess tension. We must eliminate this tension and let the internal muscles do their job. I've proven that anyone can sing without strain by allowing various doctors to study my vocal cords. The results proved that all low, high, clean, and gritty tones can be performed in a safe, healthy manner without that extra oomph some singers think is required.

STRAIN NO GAIN

If you strain, your range, quality, and power will suffer. Recalling tips from *Raise Your Voice*, don't forget to use the "NO" side-to-side movement (AKA the Windshield Wipers) when practicing. Remember, the "NO" serves a two-fold purpose:

1. If your voice cracks when you do the "NO" side-to-side movement, it proves that you are creating excess tension in the neck muscles and throat, squeezing the vocal cords and pharynx, thus constricting the sound. This movement will reveal that unnecessary tension.

2. By continuing to use the "NO" side-to-side movement when straining, you'll break free of that unnecessary tension because you cannot continue performing the "NO" with excess tension. Eventually, muscle tension dissipates when performing the "NO," the internal muscles take over, and the sound will move into your palate, producing buzz, which is a sign that you're free of excess tension.

FINDING YOUR TONE

This brings me to another method of releasing neck tension that works hand in hand with the "NO" while also helping to release your true, natural tone. This is the "YES" movement, tilting your head forward and backward as you sing. As I said, the "YES" movement not only helps to release vocal stress but also unleashes your pure vocal tone. You may notice vibrato kicking in as you tilt your head forward from backward. This is because the voice is free of tension and tone manipulation. In other words, you aren't trying to control how your tone sounds; you're just letting it happen. Be happy when that natural pitch vibrato makes an appearance, because it's a sign of vocal freedom.

Forward   **Backward**

Your goal when using the "YES" is a pure tone that doesn't crack and sounds the same both when tilting the head front and back. When it sounds the same and the vibrato kicks in, you've found your pure tone. **Finding Your Tone** So, if you think the voice has been freed by the "NO," slip in the "YES" front and back movement to double-check yourself and release that pure vocal tone.

Useful Tip: Thinking of the "NO" as Windshield Wipers

The "NO" movement is EXTREMELY important to extending your range. However, I find that most of my students tend to pause the "NO" movements at different times The "NO" MUST be a continual non-stop, fluid movement side to side. To keep the "NO" consistent (as well as the "YES") I suggest pretending it is like working the windshield wipers on your car during a downpour. The movement is fast, steady, and continual, which is exactly how the "no" must be performed in order to benefit from this little trick. If your neck stops moving, it's a sign on excess of tension in both sides of the neck. If you stop moving mid-way, and do not continue moving your head to the right side, it's a sign of excess tension in the left side of the neck. If you stop moving mid-way, and do not continue moving your head to the left side, it's a sign of excess tension in the right side of the neck.

REVISITING THE CORE OF RESONANCE

Just because we've focused on the teepee, the "YES" movement, and technique basics, don't think I forgot our old faithful core of resonance. This time around, I want my *RYV* users to dedicate more focus to their tone. After all, the end goal is a better singing voice, correct? Correct. However, just so you understand, my books are focused on vocal health and voice strengthening, not "singing artistry," which is what I cover in private lessons, Skype lessons, and the Vendera Vocal Academy, as I personally don't believe "singing artistry" can be taught in a book. Passionate singing is an art that needs to be nurtured and developed by a coach who is passionate.

But that doesn't mean I don't expect you to develop a better tone while strengthening your voice. I want you to have the best-quality sound possible so that when you walk from your strength training session into your singing session, you have a great tone to begin molding your own true voice and style.

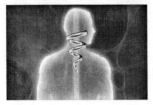

So, from now on, when thinking of that floating ball, which is your core of resonance, floating up and down within your body within the central tube, I want you to imagine that the ball in the tube has transformed into a resonating spiral, spinning resonance outwards. This shouldn't be too hard to imagine considering we all know the body is a tuning fork. Spiral that tube out of control so every fiber of your body is enhancing your overall resonance!

I think that's enough review of vocal technique. Let's move ahead to vocal health.

REVISITING VOCAL HEALTH

IT SHOULD COME AS no surprise to *Raise Your Voice* readers that I consider vocal health a major priority. Considering that we each experience different life choices that can affect our voice, we must each find our own path to vocal health. There are basic guidelines to keep the voice healthy and strong, including dietary choices, vitamins, minerals, herbs, mental attitude, and physical exercise, but our vocal health can still change in an instant, as we're affected by climate change, physical/mental stress, and allergens. What kept your voice in shape last year might not be the solution when you get sick this time around. I had to learn this truth the hard way.

In 2010, I flew to Bahrain with my guitarist, Scott Stith, to conduct a vocal performance workshop. It was a vocal nightmare. The thirteen-hour flight, hundred-degree weather, and food poisoning not only did me in physically but also scarred me emotionally.

After the bout of food poisoning in Bahrain, I had to perform on radio and television before conducting the four-hour workshop, all while feeling like a vocal wreck. I did my usual fixer elixir, doses of Emergen-C, with singer's water and zinc, yet I still suffered. A friend of mine, Anna Mercer, was kind enough to attend the workshop and bring alkaline water and ginger tea as an alternative to aid me during my affliction. It definitely helped my voice, but I was still a long way from the safe zone.

We then flew straight from Bahrain to Australia. Another thirteen-hour flight only aggravated my voice. By the time we landed, I was so dry and damaged that I could barely squeak out, "I need water." Still, I was determined to bounce back, so I kept up the fixer elixir, vocalized with *Voice RX* and *The Ultimate Vocal Warm Up* mp3s, and listened to the *Vocal Mindset* mp3s.

My work paid off. By my first Australian workshop, though I was still not back to total vocal health, I was in the zone. My students loved us, and we helped change many voices for the better.

That tour made me realize that a singer's circumstances can easily change. Now I know that I may have to turn to something other than my usual fixer elixir. Thus, I'll always continue my search for vocal health alternatives.

Since changing time zones and climates can throw the mind and body for a loop, especially when forced to keep going, as many touring artists are forced to do, always be prepared to handle any situation. If you're a touring artist, you should DEFINITELY keep a copy of *Raise Your Voice* in your gig bag, as well as the above-mentioned mp3s on standby. You never know when you'll run into a situation where you'll need to flip through my book in order to figure out what to do for any given vocal situation.

Myles Kennedy knows this to be true firsthand. He texted me while on tour with Slash to say he had a copy of *Raise Your Voice* with him just in case. If it's good enough for Myles, well …

The moral to this boring story: Always be prepared to modify your vocal health combinations. If you feel like you've tried them all and want more product alternatives and new vocal health ideas, read on.

Actually, before reading on, know that all the tips from *Raise Your Voice* always apply, but take what I give you here and expand your vocal health tip vault. As you experiment, you'll discover that one daily dose may work well for a month before it needs to be adjusted to suit your current state of vocal health. As well, some teas or sprays may not work as well for one singer as they do another. This is why you must research and experiment to find what works best for you.

With that said, I still love products like Vocal Eze and Throat Coat Tea, but as a voice-strengthening coach, it's my duty to research new vocal-related products. When I research a new product, I must stay objective because I've come across both good and bad vocal products. For instance, I once reviewed a ridiculously expensive product with outrageous vocal rejuvenation claims based on a "secret" formula. All I can say is, "I don't buy snake oil." Now let's dive into new vocal health tips, starting with a new product line that I hold dear to my heart.

SUPERIOR VOCAL HEALTH

I discovered a new line of products for singers that I now personally use. The line is called Superior Vocal Health, or SVH created by singer, cantor, vocal coach, David Aaron Katz. I such an advocate for the Superior Vocal Health line, that co-produced and published the book (via Vendera Publishing), *Superior Vocal Health*, authored, of course, by Superior Vocal Health owner David Katz.

Currently, the SVH line offers four products:

1. Sinus Clear Out—A liquid that helps to clear clogged sinus passages
2. Stage Fright—A chewable tablet that helps to relieve anxiety and stress while helping to promote mental clarity and focus
3. Throat Saver—A rapid response spray that helps to remove mucus from the cords and promotes vocal hydration
4. Vocal Rescue—A gargle to rejuvenate overused and tired voices

I've personally tested the SVH product line while performing on several television shows in China and workshops in Poland. SVH products kept my voice healthy and my mind in the zone during those shows and workshops. I'm proud to say that SVH is part of my vocal emergency health kit. Check them out at superiorvocalhealth.com.

PORTABLE STEAMING

Sprays and herbs are still important to vocal health, but water is the key to a healthy, well-oiled voice. As a singer, it is important to monitor your hydration level. One way to keep your hydration level high is by steaming. Touring artists who live their days on the road know well how hydration levels can plummet, especially when dealing with something as taxing on the voice as air conditioning. However, it's hard to pack a steamer like the Venta-Sonic on a bus or plane. Luckily, we now have the portable steamer.

Before discovering the portable steamer, I purchased a nebulizer, thinking I could inhale on the go to keep my cords moist. Unfortunately, it didn't work as well as I'd hoped. Mist inhaling proved far better, so I stuck with old faithful—my 1-ounce spray bottle. Ironically, when I was searching for an alternative, my student Ben Thomas from the band Zappa Plays Zappa was having trouble with dryness on the road. He wasn't getting what he needed from mist inhaling, so he asked me for advice. I, of course, could only suggest a steamer for the tour bus. Ben did some online research and discovered a portable steamer that

uses a 20-ounce water bottle as its water source. This was the perfect tour bus tool to humidify his bunk space.

The portable steamer is great for planes, trains, automobiles, and hotel rooms. Perform an online search for "portable steamer" to find one that suits you.

MEETING YOUR WATER QUOTA

Steaming is great, but it's not enough. Many singers fail to realize how easily water can be leached from the system. Whenever we consume drinks like coffee, soda, or beer, it easily dehydrates the vocal cords and makes it tougher to sing. In fact, David Katz said in his book, *Superior Vocal Health*, that for every can of soda we consume we need as much as thirty times the amount of water to return our body pH balance to alkaline and rehydrate the vocal cords. Therefore, I suggest tracking your water intake to keep your body well hydrated. I don't expect you to drink thirty times the amount of soda you consume, but I do expect you to begin tracking your daily water quota.

So, drink up! Make sure you drink clean, fresh water. I suggest using a BPA-free water bottle so you won't have to fear traces of plastic leaching into your water. This is why I use the water bottle from singerswater.com as well as their singer's water packets to enhance and purify my water. At home, you can add a filtration system to your water line or use a BPA-free pitcher with a built-in water purifier. There are also portable models that hook to faucets for road trips.

To calculate your basic daily water quota, revisit *Raise Your Voice* to discover the minimum amount of water per day required to stay hydrated. Divide the ounces of water required per hour by how many hours you plan to stay awake per day to figure your minimum hourly requirement. I understand that during rehearsals and gigs you will drink more water, which is perfectly fine. You need extra water when singing. And don't forget those water-heavy fruits like oranges. Choose an orange or some melon over a bag of chips. It will help to hydrate the voice, boost your energy, and satisfy your appetite. Track your daily water consumption in *The Ultimate Vocal Workout Diary.*

FYI- at this point in my life, I'm now drinking two to three times my daily water quota. My doctor suggested that I work towards a goal of three to four gallons per day due to the amount of singing and physical exercise I'm doing. Don't worry about those health myths concerning too much water. You'd need to drink ten gallons per day to wreck your body. So, it's time for you to decide if you're up to a one, two, three, or four gallon challenge. PS- anyone that tells you that you do not need much water is an idiot!

Useful Tip: Water Blasting the Throat

If you are meeting your water quota and still feel vocally dry, a great trick I use for instant hydration (besides steaming and mist inhaling) is water blasting the back of the throat. You can do this one of two ways. You can do a quick blast using Neilmed's

Sinus Rinse bottle, or use Neilmed's Singator. Simply yawn, and then blast a steady stream of water directly into the back of the throat for several seconds while breathing normally. It might feel uncomfortable at first, but eventually you'll feel a hydrating, relaxed sensation in the throat tissue. Think of water blasting as your personal throat Jacuzzi.

Useful Tip: What About Phlegm?

"But Jaime, I eat healthy, I meet my water quota, I don't feel dry, but I'm awful phlegmy, to the point it affects my singing. What is going on?" Well, you already know a lot about phlegm from *Raise Your Voice*. If you've followed the vocal health section from my first book, and you still have phlegm issues, I would wonder if Candida or infected sinuses were the culprits. First thing first—start sinus flushing several times a day using a saltwater/singer's water mix. The ionic silver in the singer's water sachet will help to kill bacteria in the sinus cavities. We want to be sure your sinuses are clean and clear of infection and not draining down the back of the throat, aggravating the vocal cords. I would also suggest a daily regimen of ten drops oil of oregano added to your bottle of Emergen-C as well as adding plain yogurt (non-flavored) to your diet In order to build up healthy bacteria in your system and to help kill a Candida overgrowth. Please research oil of oregano to learn about its amazing healing qualities and to choose the right dosage for you.

SINUS AND THROAT HEALTH

Since I've just mentioned sinuses, let's revisit sinus and throat health. Changes in weather from one extreme to the other, airborne pollutants, as well as large crowds of people, subject us to pollutants and viruses that can lead to the sniffles, scratchies, or sandpaper voice box. Colds, sinus infections, coughing, congestion, dry throat, all of which cause us to cough, sneeze, or clear our throats, are detrimental to vocal health. Here are a few tips to beat the coughing, sneezing, throat-clearing days:

Don't Cough. Yeah, I said it, just don't cough. It's easier said than done. Of course, if it's a full-blown cough, you may have to wait it out. OTC cough syrups and cough drops may suppress the symptoms by drying out the throat, so I suggest that you stay away from those remedies. Instead, crank up the steamer/humidifier and add a tablespoon of Braggs Apple Cider Vinegar to alleviate the continual coughing.

I've also used flax spray to moisten and calm irritated vocal cords. Add four or five drops of organic flax oil to an ounce of water in a 1-ounce spray bottle. Shake to mix and then spray the mist into the back of the throat as you mist inhale. It seems to lightly coat the cords, easing throat discomfort. It's important to dispose of flax spray the same day you use it as flax oil tends to spoil quickly when not refrigerated. If you have the means to refrigerate your spray, that will help to maintain it for a longer period of time. But remember that coldness tightens the cords, so remove flax spray from the refrigerator thirty minutes before using. Cradle it in your palm to warm the spray.

Upon returning from my first Chinese trip, I caught a horrible chest cold, which is rare and unusual for me. When the coughing stage hit, I didn't have any flax oil on hand, but I did have Vocal Rescue from Superior Vocal Health. It helped to soothe my voice during those harsh coughing bouts. Try my suggestions to alleviate that cough.

Don't Sneeze. When I feel a sneeze coming on I allow the pitch of my voice to go high. This keeps the sneeze from being released in a low, guttural, forced tone. A throaty sneeze may cause vocal cord swelling, because that harsh burst of air creates a smacking sensation on the vocal cords, like smacking your hands together. A high-pitched sneeze alleviates some of the forced pressure. I also flush my sinuses using a Neti pot by NeilMed.

When you feel a sneeze coming on and you don't have time to reach for a Neti pot, I suggest heading to a sink to splash your face with water. This has helped to stop my sneezing. If possible, easily clear your sinuses by blowing softly into a tissue. Heavy blowing will only aggravate the irritant that is causing your sneezing fit. If sneezing still causes problems, use Sinus Clear Out by Superior Vocal Health.

Don't Clear Your Throat. Throat clearing is a habit many singers possess; a constant "ahem" to fling the phlegm. Throat clearing is as harsh on the cords as coughing and sneezing. Coughing could be the sign of a nervous habit or lack of water. Singers need plenty of water to keep the throat moist, so make sure to meet your water quota. If you're drinking caffeinated products or alcoholic beverages, remember, both dry out the voice. So start by drinking plenty of fresh, clean water this instant. Make sure it's room temperature because cold water will tense the throat muscles.

Throat clearing can be tamed by using a humidifier while sleeping. As I mentioned earlier, portable humidifiers with 20-ounce water bottle adapters are perfect for a one-night supply of air-aqua. It may take several days to get that hydration back into the vocal cords, so you may still feel the need to clear your throat. Pay attention to your voice and consciously fight against the throat-clearing habit. When the feeling arises, fight, fight, fight against it. Remember tips from *Raise Your Voice*, such as sucking on your lower lip and lightly coughing to remove mucus buildup. This is much less taxing than clearing the throat the habitual way, which slams the cords together like smacking your hands. For immediate relief, mist inhale using flax spray. I'm hoping these tips provide you some relief. Now on to my voice stabilizer.

Useful Tip: The Voice Stabilizer

Sometimes our voices are simply worn out even without coughing, sneezing, clearing the throat, or suffering from a cold. During those times, I turn to *Voice RX*, but I've also discovered that sustaining the "V" sound helps to ease throat discomfort. I call this sound the **Voice Stabilizer** because it vibrates the palate, teeth, lips, gums, and vocal cords, acting as a "self-massage" to stabilize your pure tone and help to reduce swelling. It's somewhat similar to vocalizing through a straw. Now that you're done sneezing, coughing, wheezing, hacking, choking and have stabilized your voice, I'd like to offer another tip that will help to keep the overall body in peak condition.

Useful Tip: Maintaining and Keeping Your Energy in Peak State

Now that you're hydrated and in a perfect state of vocal health, let's discuss overall energy. I know daily life can drain you dry. I'm living proof. Many of my students who've complained of lack of energy have turned to energy drinks, pills, or five-hour energy shots. These options will only deplete your adrenals, leaching your natural energy supply. That sugar crash a few hours after doesn't mean nap time; it means it's time to find an alternative energy-boosting source.

I personally use two packets of Emergen-C and a shot of liquid ginseng as a natural alternative to an energy drink. Another alternative I've found to help combat fatigue, boost energy, and reduce stress is the Q-Link pendant. I've mentioned this product before, but it's so important to the singer that I needed to mention it once again.

Q-Link® SRT-3™ represents a new class of performance equipment that I've found helpful for musicians, given our lifestyles. It's designed to optimize the functioning of the body. Easily worn and utilized, the Q-Link pendant helps to balance and strengthen the body's energetic system, or "biofield," helping to enable peak physical, mental, and emotional capacity.

I wear Q-link products continuously, and I've given pendants to artists like Ben Thomas, Jim Gillette, and Kevin Rudolf. If you've ever been to one of my workshops or watched me sing or break glass on television, you've seen me wearing a Q-Link Silver Cross or one of the Q-Link pendants such as the titanium or basic black pendant. I truly believe Q-Link helps me contend with stress and streamlines my mind and body to help me be "in the zone" in life, particularly when I perform. It keeps my body in a healthier, energetic state, aiding in combating colds and other come-and-go ills that slow me down. If you're interested, check out singersqlink.com to learn more.

Now it's time for some physical exercise.

PHYSICAL EXERCISE

When you're a singer, you must challenge your body daily to stay in stage-ready shape. As you know, I'm a true believer in cardio as a singer's best friend. I love the programs from RMAX as well as cardio singing, as mentioned in *Raise Your Voice* and *Sing Out Loud*. I'm sure you remember my friend Ryan Murdock, who wrote an article for *Raise Your Voice* and designed the singer's exercise program, *12-Minute Stage Crazy*. Ryan also designed a new program that kicked my arse called *ShapeShifter*, which is based on the same RMAX bodyweight methods he's known for. Check it out at bodyweightburn.com.

To the point, you need to exercise. But physical exercise only works if you do it, and you'll only exercise if it maintains your interest. I've tried *P90X*, and though it was a great program, it wasn't for me. I hated the 90-minute yoga program, so I quickly lost interest. *Insanity* was better, but I fell in love with *ShapeShifter*.

Since I've completed the *ShapeShifter* program, I've moved on to other combinations of exercises to exhaust my muscles, including something I call skip bounding and a total body cardio program I've dubbed the Maximizer, because it maximizes the use of your entire body while minimizing the space and time needed to perform the routine. It's an excellent exercise for a hotel room when the only space you have for your workout is between two beds. Let's review these new exercise routines to find out if they're right for you.

Exercise #1—Skip Bounding

Skip bounding is a way to break your legs, ha-ha. Let it be known that I am NOT responsible if you fall and cannot get up. Skip bounding is basically jumping on a rebounder while using a jump rope. It's easier on your knees than running or using a jump rope on solid ground and allows you to work your upper body as well. When skip bounding, start with a basic jump rope pattern, both feet together, and aim for twenty-five skips in a row. It sounds easy, but it's awkward. Once you become accustomed to the basic skip-bounding pattern, you can change the way you skip, such as alternating the lifting of your legs, as well as increase the number of skips per session. When you're comfortable, aim for five hundred skips per session.

Exercise #2—Total Body Cardio

Total body cardio, aka the Maximizer, may seem confusing, but it's quite simple if you follow along with the descriptions and pictures below (or watch the videos in Vendera Vocal Academy SingFit classes). All the movements should flow seamlessly from one movement to the next, consisting of the following:

1. Begin with your hands pointing straight up in the air as you perform one **calf raise** before lowering your hands 90 degrees, straight out from the body as you're dropping into a...

Hands up   Hands 90°

2. **Squat.** From a squat position, lean forward on the hands, kicking the legs out behind you to assume a push-up position and then perform...

Squat   Push-up position   Push-up

3. One **push-up.** Then, on a slight jump, leap the legs forward together to a squat position, before rising back to a standing position.

Squat Position   Rising to Standing Position

4. From the standing position, lift into one calf raise, with hands straight up before dropping back into a squat.

Calf Raise   **Squat**

5. From the squat, lean backward onto the glutes, stretching backward slowly into a lying position.

On Glutes   **Leaning Back to Lying Position**

6. From the **flat-back** position, slowly bring your legs back over your upper torso into a lying **jackknife** position, and then return your legs to a lying position in preparation to perform one super-slow, **sit-up**. Attempt to touch your toes.

Flat Back   **Jackknife**   **Sit-Up**   **Touching Toes**

7. From the sit-up position, bring the upper torso back down to a lying position in a quick swinging motion for momentum so that you can kick the legs back over your body into the jackknife position. Always attempt to bring the toes to the ground behind you with the legs straight. If you cannot, you can bend at the knees.

Swinging Legs Back   **Jackknife**   **Bent Knees**

8. As soon as you assume the jackknife position, reverse the momentum by swinging the legs forward to allow your body to revert to a raised squat position, before returning to a standing position with the hands to the sky.

Jackknife Position **Raised Squat Position** **Hands to Sky**

This completes one repetition of the Maximizer. Each time you cycle through the full routine, increase the calf raises and push-ups by one count. For example, during the second set you will perform two push-ups and two calf raises each time you go into the calf raise. Third set will go to three, fourth set to four, and so on.

Perform as many sets of the Maximizer as you can. If you pause between sets, you're finished for the day. The Maximizer must be a continual, nonstop, flowing workout, whether you do two sets or twenty.

Exercise #3—Treadmill Speed Alternating

Here's one more exercise routine that might fit your needs. For those who love running on a treadmill, this is the secret to a quick, heart-pounding run in less than twenty minutes. Basically, you'll change the treadmill speeds while running every minute starting at a speed of three (3) working up to a speed of eight (8), always returning to your beginning speed on the odd minutes. The speeds would look like this:

3-4-3-5-3-6-3-7-3-8-3-7-3-6-3-5-3-4-3.

If starting at a speed of three is too fast or slow, you can decrease or increase your beginning speed to suit your current performance level. Enough long-winded vocal health tips from me. But that doesn't mean we're finished. Before ending this chapter, I want to hand it over to someone as talkative as me—David Katz of Superior Vocal Health. If anyone knows the trials and tribulations of vocal health, it's David. So, take it away, Katzy . . .

KEYS TO SUPERIOR VOCAL HEALTH
By David Aaron Katz

Being a professional singer is like being a professional athlete. You must be in the best possible shape, take care of yourself, and become very disciplined mentally. You must be willing to do whatever it takes to keep your voice healthy at all times. You must learn how to constantly be in superior vocal health. This is not an easy task, especially with being on the road, having a family, always singing in different kinds of venues and weather conditions, and dealing with age and changes in the metabolism. That is why you need to know how to take care of your vocal health and make it the number one priority in your life.

Vocal health should never be taken for granted. You'll never know when that phone call may come and you need to be ready to sing, no matter what the time of day or conditions around you.

I have been singing professionally for more than twenty years. I have had to sing under every condition imaginable, from outside in the steaming hot summer singing the National Anthem at Citi Field in New York to 30,000 screaming New Yorkers, to singing a surprise opera aria solo in a private opera box for a holiday concert with a broken foot! For me, it never mattered what the circumstance, I always made sure my throat and cords were ready to go. Then I knew that whatever scenario came to me, I would be ready.

Being in superior vocal health at all times means eating well, taking correct vitamins and supplements, getting enough rest, and not abusing your voice. However, there are times we are faced with situations that are out of our control, such as waking up with clogged sinuses the day of a performance, being overtired vocally and physically and still needing to perform, not being able to eat properly before a performance, not being able to sleep the night before a performance or show, etc. What do we do then? I am going to give you some excellent solutions to the above-mentioned scenarios. These solutions will be helpful not only for your voice but also for your overall health as well. In general, you should start taking better care of yourself today. Now is always the best time to start! Here we go.

Clogged Sinus Passages

If you wake up in the morning with clogged sinus passage and need a powerful agent to clear your sinuses here is an effective way to immediately clear out your sinuses for your presentation or performance. This is what you will need before you begin:

1. One bottle of quality eucalyptus oil, preferably organic
2. Two Q-tips
3. A warm shower

Turn on your shower to a heat you can handle without it being too hot on your skin. Put a number of towels at the bottom of the door so the steam from the shower does not escape the room. Steaming is essential for proper vocal health care, especially when your vocal apparatus and throat are under siege and your sinuses are clogged; however, this procedure will speed healing even more.

Before you get into the shower, take each Q-tip and dip it in the eucalyptus oil, making sure it is covered completely and soaked. Put the eucalyptus oil and Q-tips on a clean towel or tissue on the counter next to the shower or somewhere close so you can reach them from the shower. Before you get into the shower, spill a few drops of eucalyptus oil on the floor of the shower. Be careful how much you use; if you use too much, the oil may burn your feet.

Get into the shower. Breathe deeply and slowly, allowing the mixture to fill your lungs. Take a few minutes to let the steam and mix of eucalyptus oil begin opening up your sinus passages. Once the steam begins to open you up, take one oil-soaked Q-tip and insert it into one nostril. Very gently and slowly, slide the Q-tip up into your sinus passage, making sure it goes all the way up into your sinus passage as far as it can go. Slowly and gently twist the Q-tip to coat your entire sinus passage.

Next, slowly pull the Q-tip out as you feel the openness in your sinus cavity and the energy of the oil working. Take the other oil-soaked Q-tip and repeat with your other sinus passage.

Within thirty seconds you will probably begin to sneeze longer and stronger than you ever have before! This is the clearing power of the oil and your sinus passages expelling all the mucus and bacteria that have been clogging you up. In addition, the oil will slide down into the back of your throat opening, cleaning and clearing out any mucus or bacteria.

You may even want to do this every other day (in addition to regular Neti pot irrigation and cleansing) before a big gig or show just to keep yourself clean and wide open. I would not recommend doing it more than twice a week. It is very powerful and you do not need more than this to take care of your sinuses.

Overused and Tired Vocal Cords

Almost every singer, speaker, actor or fellow clergy with whom I have worked has on more than one occasion had to perform with a tired or overused voice and some level of mucus on the cords. It seems to be part of our job description. As stated before, whether it's an audition, presentation, performance, or sermon, we need to be in top vocal form. However, life's responsibilities simply don't disappear when we need to be "on."

For a myriad of reasons, our voice may be ragged and tired and we still need to bring the voice up and out of our bodies with a full, confident, clear, and powerful sound. Below you may find some outstanding natural alternatives for proper vocal health care for tired and overused vocal cords that I, for one, have been using for many years. These alternatives will energize and rejuvenate your voice and throat naturally. They work almost immediately, help to restore and remove mucus from the cords and throat, and best of all, they have no side effects.

There are a number of herbs that can provide instant relief for the tired throat and vocal cords. These may be used in extract form (liquid) as a gargle or as a tea. I prefer to gargle because the herbs go directly into the throat, removing unwanted mucus and debris, providing me with immediate relief. Teas tend to pass through the throat more quickly, and contact to the affected area is not as dramatic. In addition, the herbal content in most tea bags is considerably less than that in an extract.

Also, for general vocal health care, the heat in the throat can be an effective healing agent, thereby relaxing the inflamed area. If you do purchase these herbs as teas, drink them hot with some honey. Adding lemon can be helpful, but too much citrus can dry the throat and cords. Be careful of the amount you use. One squeeze should suffice.

The following herbal combination is one of the best remedies I have used when in a clutch scenario and I am vocally wiped out but still have to go on. It is a combination of the herbal extracts ginger, cayenne, slippery elm, turmeric, and sage. I know most of you are screaming "what about licorice?!!" I am not suggesting anyone use licorice, because they may have high blood pressure. And those with high blood pressure should never take licorice. If you want to add licorice, do so on your own account and always check with your health-care provider beforehand. Each of these herbs has exceptional properties that help reduce swelling, inflammation, and pain. This combination has also been used successfully for laryngitis and hoarseness. Each individual herb can be found at any health food store but use the nonalcoholic brands. The alcohol content in certain extracts is usually quite high and can dry the throat and vocal cords, not to mention affecting brain focus.

Making a solution to gargle is very easy. Simply follow the steps below:

1. Fill a cup with two ounces of warm water. Make sure it is warm and not hot. You do not want to do more damage by burning your throat and vocal cords!
2. Add one-half to a full dropper of each extract to the water. If you have purchased a two-ounce bottle, the dropper will be larger. For two-ounce bottles of extract use half a dropper.
3. Mix in a half tablespoon of honey.
4. Gargle three times for about thirty seconds, making sure to allow the herb mixture to go as far down into your throat as possible so you get

the full impact on the cords. Then spit out the gargle mixture. Do not swallow. Swallowing small amounts will not harm you in any way except that it may make you a bit nauseous.

Do this three to five times a day on the day of your performance or every two hours. Then gargle one last time just minutes before singing.

If you don't have your mixture of herbs, one thing you can do is eat pineapple in between sets or intermission. I make sure I have a small container of pineapple backstage when I perform. Pineapple is nature's provider of bromelain. Bromelain is an enzyme mixture that has high anti-inflammatory properties. In Germany it's used medicinally for the treatment of inflamed sinuses due to surgery as well as arthritis.

Eating pineapple between sets or at intermission will help your vocal cords and throat by reducing any inflammation or swelling caused by overtiredness or pushing on the voice. In addition, pineapple will provide you with some good energy.

Natural Energy When Physically Tired

Without adequate energy all of the above-mentioned remedies will be of little or no value. The best forms of energy we have is in the food we eat and the thoughts we think. Your nutritional decisions on a regular basis will determine your overall effectiveness as a performer. Very few professional or semiprofessional singers have the luxury of resting the voice and body all day before a performance, eating perfectly, and staying quiet. Because of this fact, you must not take proper nutrition for granted. You need the most effective and powerful fuel you can get. Below you will find some excellent foods that provide outstanding energy without creating mucus or making you feel bloated, nervous, or groggy. Most of them take little or no preparation and can easily be taken with you and stored in a fridge at work or an ice pack container if you are unable to get home before you sing. You may also find a couple of my favorite "power drinks" that have served me very well over the years. Let's start with the Green Monster.

I call this the Green Monster because it really is a monster of a drink when it comes to providing the body and voice with tons of natural energy and mental clarity. It is one of my favorite and most effective total-energy, body-booster and brain-stimulating drinks. I like to make up two bottles of the Green Monster before I sing. One I drink preshow, the other midshow. This keeps me fully charged the entire show. Here's what you will need:

1. One 8- to 12-ounce bottle of filtered water or coconut water
2. One teaspoon of spirulina
3. Two scoops of "kyo-greens" (or an equivalent) green powder mixture

4. Two Emergen-C packets, your choice of flavor
5. A full dropper of ginkgo biloba or gotu cola or ginseng nonalcoholic extract
6. One tablespoon of soy lecithin
7. A dash (one small pinch) of cayenne pepper (optional for those who have trouble with spices)

Use any bottled water you may be able to find. The best would be filtered from your house, but if you are on the run, any good bottled water will do. Coconut water is a fabulous drink that tastes good and is full of vitamins and nutrients, including potassium. Potassium is what we need to maintain good solid energy levels.

For those of you unfamiliar with it, spirulina is one of the most amazing foods on our planet and is literally a "super food." It is a blue-green algae found in warm alkaline freshwater bodies. It is most often the "protein of choice" for vegetarians because it is 65 to 71 percent complete protein, with all essential amino acids in perfect balance. In comparison, beef is only 22 percent protein.

Spirulina is also loaded with beta-carotene. Spirulina has a high level of chlorophyll, which cleans and purifies the body, keeping our throats and voice crystal clear and free of mucus and phlegm, allowing for the energy to flow more smoothly and freely throughout the body. Spirulina also has plenty of vitamin B. One teaspoon of spirulina supplies two-and-a-half times the Recommended Daily Allowance of vitamin B12 and contains over twice the amount found in an equivalent serving of liver. Vitamin B is essential for combating stress and helps calm the nervous system. Essentially, spirulina energizes, clears, and stimulates the brain and body all at once.

Emergen-C is a small, convenient powdered vitamin C packet that every voice professional should never be without. There are 1000 mg of vitamin C in every packet as well as 200 mg of potassium, another energy-producing supplement. They come in different flavors and taste great.

Ginkgo biloba, ginseng, and gotu cola are herbs that stimulate the brain and body, improving mental function and enhancing blood circulation. I know some of you are thinking, "Wow, I'm going to use all three and really fire myself up!" I do not suggest doing this. One herb is enough!

Soy lecithin is produced mainly from vegetable sources as well as soybeans. It is known as a "brain food" because it has been shown to improve memory and reaction time. It also helps improve physical performance and muscle endurance.

None of these ingredients need refrigeration, although I personally think this drink tastes better and more palatable when cold. Keep all the ingredients in your bag or purse on a regular basis. You never know when you may need them.

As mentioned, you can keep the contents right inside your bag and make it in seconds without the need for refrigeration. You won't crash thirty minutes after you drink it, have a buildup of mucus in your throat, or fog in your brain. You will have more than enough excellent energy and clarity for your show, and your body will not feel full or bloated before singing.

Another benefit of this drink is that it is a total meal replacement. In fact, you probably do not get nearly the nutritional content in your regular meals that you will receive from this one drink. To make the drink, pour all the above contents into your water bottle and shake the bottle vigorously.

Note: Be careful not to get the green powder or spirulina on your clothes. It can make a rather unattractive stain!

Another great drink is Green Tea Power. This drink mixture is a little different in its composition. It is still an excellent drink for clear, even energy and mental clarity but is a bit less involved to prepare. Here's what you will need:

1. One cup of hot water for boiling tea
2. One bag of organic green tea from Yogi Teas is excellent. If you are on the run, "China Green Tips" from Starbucks will do. You may also use two tea bags if you want a slightly more supportive caffeine boost, but be careful, because excessive caffeine usage can dry out the vocal cords and dehydrate the body.
3. One tablespoon of raw propolis extract
4. Ginseng extract (As always, organic is best.)
5. Ginger extract

Green tea is full of antioxidants that help to keep your system clean and your immune system strong and healthy. It also has a small amount of caffeine in it. Not enough to tax the nervous system but just enough to give you a quiet and easy energy lift. In addition, green tea is a primary source of theanine. Theanine is an amino acid that helps reduce stress and anxiety without making you tired or groggy. Theanine has been given to children with ADD to help them focus and relax at the same time, two very important factors we need to experience if we want to sing free and well.

Propolis is a resinous mixture that honeybees collect from tree buds, sap flows, or other botanical sources. This amazing natural medicine has been touted as having as many or more antibacterial properties as penicillin and is also a fabulous source of natural energy. It is excellent for reducing swelling in the throat, breaking up mucus in the sinuses, relieving hoarseness, and fighting infection in the throat.

Ginseng is a natural energy booster.

Ginger is one of the best overall body tonics in the herb kingdom. It stimulates the entire body. It also adds "fire" and support to the lungs, warming them. Every singer is always in need of this type of support.

If you're on the run or have no time to prepare the Green Monster or Green Tea Power, the following foods do wonders for your overall energy:

1. Goji berries
2. Dried fruits. For example, mangos are loaded with potassium, and pineapple contains bromelain, which helps to heal inflammation.
3. Raw energy bars (not power bars or protein bars)
4. Hard-boiled eggs
5. Beans and lentils
6. Sprouts
7. Broccoli, asparagus, spinach
8. Brown rice
9. Watermelon and banana
10. Freshly squeezed vegetable juice

Besides the obvious nutritional requirements, natural, deep sleep is a priority for all singers. Lack of a good night's sleep can be one of the most detrimental things to the voice. No matter how well you take care of yourself, if you do not get enough sleep, your voice will not respond well. So how do we get a good night's sleep when we are nervous, full of anxious energy, or just full of excitement for the show? OTC is not the answer.

Taking prescription sleeping pills can negatively impact the health of your voice and body. You'll almost always wake up groggy, dry, and feeling "out of it." This leads us to drink excess caffeine or some other chemical substance to wake up enough to get started. In addition, serious mental and physical side effects have been documented due to taking prescription sleeping pills, including a potential for addiction, digestive troubles, nausea, constipation, parasomnias, delirium, tremors, and seizures.

Before you consider aiding your sleep with natural alternatives, you may want to address why you are not getting the sleep you need. Feeling excited and fired up before the night of a performance is a very natural and normal thing most all professional artists go through. However, if it is more than preshow excitement, you may need to address the issue. Some things that affect a good night's sleep are:

1. Drinking excess amounts of caffeine—five or more cups throughout the day or after 7:00 pm

2. Eating a large and difficult-to-digest meal after 7:00 pm or before you go to sleep
3. Eating refined sugar or candy before you go to sleep
4. Using your computer for more than a half hour to an hour before you go to sleep
5. Exercising vigorously before you go to sleep

If these situations are not the culprit and you simply need a little support for sleeping, here are a few of my favorite natural sleep aids:

1. Borage—Borage has been called the "Tea of Courage" because of the calming effects it has on the body and mind, allowing the user to be less nervous or anxious. It is fantastic for calming the entire nervous system. If you have trouble going to sleep, a nice strong cup of borage tea before going to bed can provide a very restful sleep with no grogginess or "feeling out of it" in the morning. Borage is very strong. Try small amounts first to see how your body reacts. Borage may be purchased in bulk leaf form or in a liquid dropper. If you cannot find the bulk form locally, look online. When using fresh herb as a tea, bring two cups of water to boil. Add one tablespoon of fresh herb. Let boil for three minutes. Take off heat and let sit covered for ten minutes. Strain and drink warm.

2. Catnip—It's not just for felines. Catnip is generally used as a mood elevator. It is helpful for tension and stress, aids in insomnia, affords a general feeling of well-being, and is excellent for alleviating anxiety and nervousness. Catnip has also been used for centuries as an excellent overall pain reliever. Many people use catnip as a natural alternative to over-the-counter sleeping pills. It is very strong and can be used regularly without any feeling of waking up groggy or tired in the morning. Two or three capsules one half hour before bedtime will certainly afford a good night's sleep. A nice tea may also be used. Boil two cups of water and then allow the water to simmer down for a few minutes. Never boil catnip. It will render the herb useless. Add one tablespoon of herb, freshly cut if possible, or powder after the boiling water is removed from the heat source. Let steep covered for twenty minutes, drain, and then drink. Catnip is not the tastiest herb when used as a tea. Some honey may be added to make it more palatable. If you do not have fresh herb, you may also add a half dropper of liquid extract to a cup of warm water twenty minutes before bedtime.

3. Chamomile—Chamomile has a calming effect on the entire body. While not as powerful as some of the other herbs, such as valerian, skullcap, or lobelia, it is good for soothing the stomach and for mild nervousness. It has been known to ease the pain of migraine headaches as well. Chamomile can be taken and used effectively in almost any form of tea, powder, capsule, or crushed plant. Known in the West mostly for its soothing qualities, chamomile is actually a stimulant with antispasmodic properties. It is one of the most popular herbs taken as a tea to help soothe the stomach. However, it is also excellent for a number of other ailments, including bronchitis, colds, allergies, and headaches caused by tension and stress. A strong cup twenty minutes before bedtime should do the trick.

4. Hops—Hops is a well-known herb used for insomnia, nerves, anxiousness, and even an overabundance of sexual energy. Hops is very effective at relaxing the entire nervous system. Try this "old-fashioned" remedy for insomnia. Take a small batch of fresh hops flowers and stuff your pillow before going to bed. Then have a cup of hops tea. This is said to give one a very restful sleep. (Hops should not be used by people who take antidepressants)

5. Melatonin—Melatonin is a hormone made by the pineal gland, a small gland in the brain. Melatonin is your body's natural way of helping to control your sleep and wake cycles. Small amounts, not really enough to affect sleep, can be found in foods such as meats, grains, fruits, and vegetables. Your body will slow down its melatonin production when light comes into the area you are sleeping in. To take full advantage of your own melatonin production, sleep in a dark room and make sure no light can slip in. Melatonin production also decreases with age. So depending on how old you are, you should check with your health-care provider as to how much you should take. Melatonin can be very effective. If you decide to take it, monitor yourself very carefully for potential side effects that can arise from a dosage level that is too high for your body. These can include sleepiness, lower body temperature, some small changes in blood pressure, and dreams that seem a bit out of the ordinary.

6. Passion flower—Passion flower has been used regularly for its calming, sedative, and pain-relieving actions. It is also used by herbalists to treat anxiety, insomnia, muscle spasms, stress, headaches, seizures, hysteria, and hyperactivity in children. Passion flower's unique calming quality works so well because of how it affects

the nervous system. It tones the sympathetic nerves and improves blood circulation and the nutrition that the nerves receive. In the United States, passion flower has been banned because of claims that the herb's ability to effectively do what its proponents claim has gone unproven. However, in Europe it is widely used on a regular basis for the above issues, particularly as a mild sedative and non-addictive tranquilizer. Passion flower can be a safe, reliable remedy to performance anxiety and stage fright or insomnia due to nerves the night before a performance. Add two tablespoons of passion flower to a pint of boiling water. Reduce heat and let sit covered for fifteen minutes. Strain and drink. If you do not have fresh herb, you may also use liquid extract. Add half a dropper of liquid extract of passion flower into a warm cup of chamomile tea. If you need more, add as you wish. Try passion flower first in small doses to see how it affects you. (Do not take passion flower with MAO-inhibiting antidepressants or during pregnancy or lactation, as its safety during these times has not yet been determined.)

7. Skullcap—Skullcap is one of the most powerful nerve tonics in the herbal kingdom and can be compared with catnip, valerian, and lobelia. When combined with other nerve tonic herbs, it is useful for diseases of the nervous system. Since the early days in Western herbal medicine it has been used as a nerve tonic and sedative. When taken in the proper dosage levels it will produce a deep and long sleep with no side effects in the morning. It is also very good for headaches, muscle spasms, and irritability. Some herbalists have used skullcap for helping people with addictions to drugs, alcohol, and cigarettes. It may be used safely on a long-term basis for helping with regulation of the nervous system. A good introductory dose would be ten drops of extract in two ounces of water before bedtime. Do not use while driving. Some companies have mislabeled their products as skullcap. Be careful to not use mislabeled skullcap products, as they have been shown to cause liver damage.

8. Valerian root—Valerian, or "valeriana," comes from the Latin *valere*, which means "to be in good health." Along with St. John's root, valerian is one of the first herbs prescribed by herbalists because it is one of the best nerve-calming herbs. It has even been called "nature's tranquilizer." It is a safe and effective sedative that can be very useful for hysteria, nervous tension, stress, and insomnia. It is believed that the relief partly derives from valerian's supposed ability to slightly reduce blood pressure. Upon first use, try valerian alone in increasing

doses to see how it works for you. However, in some people it can have the opposite effect, acting as a stimulant. If this is the case, discontinue use and try one of the other nerve-calming herbs. If you choose to use valerian, begin with one half dropper of extract in a cup of warm water. You may want to add a small amount of honey for taste. Valerian tea can also be used but may not be as concentrated as the extract dose. To make your own tea, use one teaspoon of dry herb in a cup of hot water. Boil for three minutes, let steep for twenty minutes covered. Strain and drink. This will be a very strong cup of tea. Another plus for using valerian as a sleep aid is that it does not interact negatively with alcohol. (Valerian should not be taken for more than two weeks at a time. Consult with a qualified herbalist before using valerian.)

Being a cantor, teacher, and full professional singer, I understand the extraordinary demands put on the voice professional. Our craft is a complete mental, physical, and spiritual one. We need to take care of ourselves, and many times, more so than not, we need additional support. Getting it from the right food sources is key. You have the choice to decide how you will take care of your voice. Choosing wisely and effectively will ensure a joyous and successful career. As always, I wish you the best on your quest for Superior Vocal Health.

David Aaron Katz is the CEO and founder of Superior Vocal Health. He is also a nutritional consultant, herbalist, and the author of the internationally read blog "Superior Vocal Health." He has been singing opera and Broadway music internationally for more than 22 years.

He has sung with many prominent symphonies in the United States including the Pan American Symphony of New York, The Atlanta Symphony, and the Houston Grand Opera Symphony with Marvin Hamlisch conducting. Mr. Katz has committed his entire career to helping fellow singers take care of their voices naturally without chemicals or drugs. Learn more at superiorvocalhealth.com.

Useful Tip: 7-Day Vocal Juicing to Reset the Voice

David definitely knows his stuff when it comes to vocal health. Following in his footsteps, here is a GREAT way to help reset a voice that is tired, dry, and generally worn. Be forewarned, it isn't for the weak. Basically, we're going to start a 7-day juice fast to feed the voice nutrients to help clean up your tone and clear out phlegm.

As a replacement for breakfast, lunch, dinner, and any snacks in between, juice in a juicer and drink the following:

Four leaves of Kale
Large handful of Spinach
Two stalks of Celery
Two green apples
One large carrot
1/2 peeled lemon
One inch of fresh ginger root
One cucumber
Two Fresh slices of pineapple
Two ounces of Aloe Vera Juice

The drink is delicious and you can drink as much as you need to fill you up. Be prepared, you may feel hungry and tired and want to quit the fast, but try to stick with it. Your voice will feel much better by the end of the fast!

Useful Tip: SVH Daily Vocal Maintenance

To enhance your daily vocal maintenance program, I suggest gargling a full dropper of Vocal Rescue in a few ounces of warm water followed by placing a full dropper of Sinus Clear Out under your tongue for ten seconds before swallowing, first thing in the morning. I also suggest sticking a copy of David's book, *Superior Vocal Health* in your gigbag alongside of *RYV1 & RYV2*.

Phew, enough about vocal health; let's revisit something else...

3

Revisiting the Ultimate Vocal Warm-Up

B EFORE REHEARSAL, VOICE LESSONS, vocal workshops, and television appearances, I ALWAYS warm up! Why? Because I'm not a natural; I have to work for it and I'd prefer to have my voice my entire life. Before diving into new warm-ups, I have a golden piece of advice for you—regardless of your warm-up routine, take your warm-up one note at a time! Now, I know that sounds soooo simple, but you wouldn't believe how many singers fail to properly warm up because they either rush through the routine and don't allow time for the blood flow to increase to the vocal cords, or they push too high without letting the lower notes come to fruition before working the voice higher. Both are major mistakes. So, when I warm up, whether with my TUNED XD pitch wheel, at a keyboard, or with an mp3, I never work higher in my range until I feel the lower and midrange notes coming freely. Case in point, I did Lip Bubbles for several hours on the morning of my first television show, *Good Morning America.* After a night of screaming at glasses, all it took was me slowly taking my time to get the blood flow to my cords and open my voice for those high notes. By show time early that morning, I was in the zone! I was experiencing the Crystal Voice Phenomenon. (See VenderaVocalAcademy.com to learn more about the CVP.)

Over the years, my warm-ups have varied, but I always perform Vocal Stress Release followed by one of my warm-up mp3s such as *The Ultimate Vocal Warm* Up, *voice* RX, or *The Rock & Metal Singer's Warm Up Routine* to break the monotony of major scales and get me in the rock mood. I also add in a few E-Screams before my glass-breaking performances. My point is that I never hit the stage unprepared.

I've met many singers who complain of performance inconsistencies, and nine times out of ten it's because they didn't warm up or they didn't take it one note at a time. So, ALWAYS do Vocal Stress Release, followed by the warm-up routine of your choice. Since this is the advanced manual, I'd like to offer a few new warm-up tips to maximize your preshow warm-up routine.

Useful Tip: Which warm-up do I use???

Before moving on, I should probably cover the warm-up programs that I have created one more time to end any confusion you might have over which to use. People have asked me again and again which program is best. Is it best to follow the exact warm-up approach described in *Raise Your* Voice, or is it better to slightly modify to use the *Beyond the Ultimate Vocal Warm Up* video from my *Beyond the Voice* series? Or is the 15-minute *Ultimate Vocal Warm Up* mp3 the better choice? Is *Voice RX* better than *The Rock & Metal Singer's Warm Up Routine?* All good questions. But there's no correct answer.

Truth be told, all my programs are based on the same approach but vary to offer variety. So, in my opinion, it's best to mix up the routines to keep from becoming bored. They will all serve the same purpose. Personally, I use different programs on different days. As I said earlier, I always perform VSR, then one of my warm-up routines. Most mornings, I warm up in the shower with an mp3. For my shower routine, I only use *Voice RX* if my voice feels under the weather. Otherwise, I alternate between the *Ultimate Vocal Warm Up* and the *Rock & Metal* mp3s so that I can bounce back and forth between major and minor scales. I also create and record a variety of different warm up scales using my TUNED XD app.

Useful Tip: Voice RX/Vocal Stress Release Combo

My student Ben Carroll (lead vocalist/guitarist of the Hollow Glow and guitarist for RA) has been using my warm-ups for years. He discovered that if he vocalized along with *Voice RX* while he was performing Vocal Stress Release, it warmed up his voice quicker and more effectively. Following his lead, I followed suit using my other mp3s. I suggest you begin doing the same. However, if you were paying attention to the paragraph above, you'll remember that I use my mp3s in the shower. Sooooo, for a super-powered vocal awakening, turbo-charging warm-up, do VSR while vocalizing to one of the mp3s while taking a hot shower. The steam will open your lungs, hydrate your cords, and loosen your muscles.

If you are a Mindset user (the program from my *Mindset* book), you can perform the Mind/Body process upon waking, right before hopping into the shower for your warm-up. This prepares your voice for the day and gets your voice used to the habit of waking up the voice early. This is especially important for singers who must conduct morning interviews and sing on morning radio shows.

Again, it doesn't matter whether you're using a pitch wheel or TUNED XD for Isolation warm-ups, or vocalizing along with the *Voice RX, Ultimate Vocal Warm Up,* or the *Rock & Metal* mp3s, just as long as you're vocalizing as you stretch and massage the body.

Useful Tip: Perfect Lip Bubbles

Regardless of the warm-up routine you choose, make sure you have those Lip Bubbles down pat. My students know I'm a stickler for perfect Lip Bubbles. For some, Lip Bubbles are extremely difficult. Luckily for them, I've discovered a way to make Lip Bubbles easier. By thinking as if the energy of the voice originates right behind the lips during Lip Bubbles instead of down in the throat, you'll physically feel the vocal tone being produced on the front side of the teeth landing against the lips. This takes more stress off the cords, minimizes breath release, and makes it easier to perform Lip Bubbles. It doesn't negate palate resonance, though the strong lip vibration does tend to overpower the sensation of palate buzz, making you think you've lost placement. I assure you that you have not. Confused? Just pretend the front of your teeth are tiny lungs producing the breath, and you'll feel what I'm talking about. This sensation actually works for other exercises as well. For example, if you pretend that the soft palate is the source of vocal energy (breath) when Gargling Tone, it will minimize breath pressure and feel much easier. It's the same with all the vowels as you are vocalizing, and coincides with the inhalation sensation as explained in *Raise Your Voice.* As you feel the inhalation sensation as you vocalize, it can feel as if it is occurring on the lips for Lip Bubbles and Resonant Hums and on the palate for Gargling Tone and other exercises.

Now that you've warmed up by vocalizing while performing VSR in the shower, let me introduce you to a new warm-up exercise that has worked well for lots of my students.

MINI-SIRENS

I felt it important to offer this one bonus warm-up that can actually help strengthen your midrange and improve your tone for my singers who prefer the "Isolation" approach to warming up. I call it the Mini-Siren. I began using it when working with my friend and Dream Theater vocalist James LaBrie. I knew he had ruptured both vocal cords due to food poisoning, so I wanted to tread lightly as we worked out his voice. Instead of full-on Sirens, I had James work Sirens in fifths, as opposed to full octaves, focusing less on range and loud volume and more on maintaining a constant buzz in the palate. We started on his lowest note and worked up only as high as he could maintain the buzz in the palate. If the buzz began to slip away or lessen, we didn't work any higher. We worked through the five vowels as follows:

Yah as in Father
Yay as in Play
Yee as in Sweet
Yoh as in Toe
You as in Food

Listen to the **Mini-Siren** example and begin adding it to your morning warm-up regimen. You don't need to repeat all five vowels per pitch. Simply start on your lowest comfortable note (vocal fry doesn't count) on a "Yah," move up a half step, switching to "Yay," and so on. Once you've completed a series of five notes and vowels, you've finished one round, or in workout terms, one set. Only work up as many sets as comfortable. Once you begin losing the buzz, stop the warm-up and don't force the voice to go higher. Like the Siren, you can do this exercise loud if you prefer, but you should maintain the volume, not getting louder. The resonant power of the Mini-Siren is so effective that it is the official exercise for my book, *SingFit.*

James later told me how important this one exercise was to his vocal routine. He also mentioned how he regularly performs his entire set by light singing (singing on as tiny volume as audible without noticeable breathiness, as explained in *Raise Your Voice*) each song acapella.

Bonus: If you want to kick this exercise up a notch, try expanding the Mini-Siren by sliding first to the third, then the fifth, and last the octave. The pattern would be 1-3-1-5-1-8-1. This would be similar to the vocal cord stretch exercise from *RYV.* If you can slip in another octave, you'd be performing the **Advanced Vocal Cord Stretch** exercise, which will stretch and warm the vocal cords in no time flat.

Useful Tip: Resetting the Voice with Elephants
Even with Mini-Sirens, vocal cord stretches, Vocal Stress Release, warm-up mp3s, and even steaming, there will be times when your voice will feel as if it is still unwilling to cooperate. A way to kick-start an unruly voice is an exercise from the *Sing Out Loud* series, which I call the Elephant exercise. **Elephants** work wonders with resetting the voice, smoothing out those cracks and reestablishing your seamless range. If you've warmed up but still feel disconnection in the voice, try a round of ten elephants. (They're more effective when done through a straw into a bottle of water.)

Generally, after a few runs, the voice starts to come back. Don't be afraid of how loud you sound as it will not hurt your voice if you breathe, support, and place correctly. Always keep the mouth shut like when humming, and focus on that strong, resonant feeling against your lips as you slide from low to high, imitating an elephant.

VOCAL STAGE PREP
Now that you've learned a few new vocal warm-up tricks, let's revisit Vocal Stress Release. If you want to take VSR to the next level and create a burst of energy to pump up your performance, Vocal Stage Prep (VSP) is the answer. VSP can be

conducted after or combined with VSR as a way to get the blood flowing throughout the entire body. Guitarists, keyboardists, and drummers are singers too, so it's time to address the overall musician's needs by adding the following routine:

1. Hand Flexor

The Hand Flexor will loosen the wrist and fingers to prepare the hands for playing an instrument. Stretch the hand forward, then backward as shown in the pictures below.

Stretch at your own pace and do not stretch beyond the point of pain. Repeat for both hands. Next, assume a prayer position with the fingers and thumbs wide.

Follow by stretching the webs between each finger and then bending each finger forward and back.

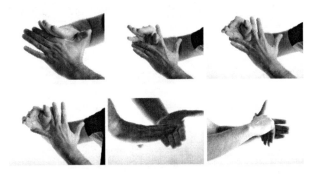

To end the Hand Flexor, massage the palm of each hand, digging deep with the opposite thumb to relieve all tension. Close the Hand Flexor by massaging the wrist and then squeezing the outside of the meaty part of the lower palm in toward the middle.

2. Windmills

Windmills wake the arms and get blood flowing into the hands. Spin your arms forward ten to fifteen times as fast as you can and then backwards ten to fifteen times parallel or 180 degrees apart as you spin.

3. Wiper Blades

Swing the hands and arms side to side, across the body, opening up the shoulders and elbows. Alternate left and right arms on top with every wiper blade. Perform this exercise ten to fifteen times.

4. Body Copters

Keep your legs locked as you spin your upper body clockwise using your hips as a stationary base. Perform ten to fifteen times. Repeat counterclockwise. You can place your hands on your hips for balance.

5. Leg Lifters

Balancing on one leg, use your hands beneath your knee to pull your other leg up into your chest for a deep stretch. Hold for five to ten seconds before switching legs.

6. Calf Stretch

Leaning forward against a wall for support, bend one leg while extending the other leg backwards. Bring the extended leg up on your toes, and then push off the wall with your hands to push the heel of the extended foot backwards to stretch the calf muscle. Repeat with opposite leg.

7. Body Primer

Finish VSP by bouncing up and down as if jumping on a trampoline for a full sixty seconds to get your heart racing and body primed for the show. Allow the arms to bounce instead of remain stationary.

Useful Tip: More Jaw Tension Release

Motor Mouths, as I call them, are another way to release jaw tension. I didn't include it above with VSP because it doesn't apply to everyone. If you have a lot of tension in your jaw, you can perform the Motor Mouth exercise right after the Jaw Tension Release in VSR to help lessen the tightness in your jawline. Basically, you create ten circles with your lower jaw, moving your jaw to the left, down, and back up to where the mouth is nearly closed. Then perform ten more circles in the opposite direction.

Finish by moving the lower jaw side to side ten times. I created Motor Mouths on the spot when one of my German students was struggling with jaw tension during singing. Thanks, Stan☺

THE VOICE & BODY COOL-DOWN

Now that you're warmed up, you should feel vocal adrenaline coursing through your rock 'n' roll veins. Once the jig is up, uh, I mean the gig is up, don't forget to cool down. But hey, wait a minute; I've redesigned your cool-down too! The Voice & Body Cool Down (VBCD) is a great tool for releasing stress in the mind and body to wind down right after the show.

I've noticed that most singers fail to cool down or only cool down for a few seconds after a performance. The VBCD will force you to finish your entire cool-down because the VBCD combines vocalization with stretching and breathing. VBCD is one flowing move, as follows:

1. As you inhale, bring your hands up toward the ceiling, rising on the tips of your toes, feeling your ribs expand.

2. Bring your hands back down as you exhale on Lip Bubbles. Slowly move to the floor (continuing your Lip Bubbles) until you are flat on the floor on your stomach with the tips of the toes on the floor and palms to your side, flat on the floor with elbows bent outward. Lip Bubbles should not end until you've established this position.

3. Raise your torso with your hands, inhaling while stretching the abdominals.

4. Begin Resonant Hums as you fold back into a child's pose.

5. Raise your body to a kneeling position on an inhale.

6. Using your hands and legs, slowly begin to rise to a standing position while exhaling on resonant Zzzs.

7. Once you've reached a standing position, drop your hands to your sides and repeat the entire process as needed.

Performing the VBCD will provide a few minutes of "me" time before you are overrun with fans and interview requests. Now that you're warmed up and cooled down, let's move onto the next chapter—the sole reason you bought this book—the Ultimate Isolation Exercise.

4

REVISITING THE ISOLATION METHOD

W E'VE FINALLY ARRIVED AT THE true purpose of this book. Welcome to THE Ultimate Isolation Exercise, my unique method for combining your warm-up and your workout routine into one exercise. I'm assuming you're fully comfortable with Lip Bubbles, Resonant Hums, Gargling Tones, Falsetto Slides, Transcending Tones, and Sirens by now. And I'm assuming you have a minimum of two octaves. If not, return to *Raise Your Voice*, because you're not ready for this book!

Note: Before you get started, check out TunedXD.com to grab TUNED XD. The 7-octave pitch wheel or pre-programmed exercises can be used for this exercise.

THE ULTIMATE ISOLATION EXERCISE

Now it's time to dive into the new methodology. The order in which I stack these exercises must NOT change, because the order will allow the voice to warm up first by focusing your sound forward, toward the lips, and then slightly moving the buzz back onto the palate while maintaining focus on the lips, and then moving from the lips entirely to the palate before beginning the Isolation workout. Once we enter workout mode, we'll barrel through the main vowel formations so that our facial muscles and oral cavity both develop the muscle memory needed for each of the five vowels while building vocal muscle and training the voice to perform each vowel on any note without vowel modification.

You might ask why I didn't include the resonant Zzzs in this exercise. That's because I use the "Z" consonant in VBCD as well as with the original and advanced versions of *Jim Gillette's Vocal Power* scales. (Though I'm trying to help you cut practice time, monster singers will want to continue using these amazing vocal scales. So, you can get your dose of Zzzs from your scales.)

Note: This is your #1 vocal strengthening exercise, but it does NOT replace your morning shower, pre-gig, or pre-rehearsal warm-up. Continue using the warm-up of choice first thing in the morning and before gigs, rehearsals, and recording sessions. When vocal strength training, use the Ultimate Isolation Exercise. No pre-warm-up besides VSR will be required, because the Ultimate Isolation Exercise simultaneously warms up the voice during each pitch as you perform your workout. Now back to your previously scheduled program …

Let me start by giving you the whole picture. The Ultimate Isolation Exercise is performed on a circle or a figure eight. This might sound bizarre unless you've watched one of my *Beyond the Voice* videos. Basically, this is a way to smoothly cover one or two octaves by visualization.

Think of the very top and bottom of a circle as an octave apart, the top being the higher octave, while the bottom of the circle is down one octave. By visualizing your voice flowing around the circle, you can smoothly slide from one octave to the next without any annoying breaks or cracks. The circle is used with individual Isolation exercises when sliding down/up one octave and when a singer is still working with less than three octaves. The true Ultimate Isolation Exercise uses a figure eight pattern to incorporate two octaves. If you're a *Raise Your Voice* user, I'm assuming you've built a solid three octaves by now, so this two-octave pattern should be a breeze. By following a figure eight on its side (like an infinity sign), you can place an octave in the center of the figure eight (point of reference) where the lines cross, one octave higher to the right at the outer edge, and one octave lower than the center octave all the way to the left at the outer edge of the figure eight.

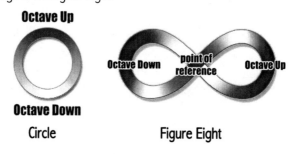

Octave Up

Octave Down

Octave Down   point of reference   Octave Up

Circle   Figure Eight

I know it sounds confusing and you may wonder why I didn't call the figure eight an infinity sign. For me, a figure eight has always clicked because I always think of an ice skater flawlessly performing a figure eight on the ice. No, I'm not an ice skating fan, though I did love *Blades of Glory,* ha-ha.

The true reason I choose to visualize a figure eight on its side is my fear that a singer might mentally picture an **8**, which runs vertically, and the singer might strain to reach the top note by thinking "up" for the highest note. Therefore I laid the figure eight on its side so we'd think "side to side" like we did in *Raise Your Voice* with the piano visualization, leaning right for the highs and left for the lows.

To perform the Ultimate Isolation Exercise on a figure eight, follow these steps:

1. Starting on C below middle C, perform the figure eight pattern on Lip Bubbles, sliding down an octave, then back to the center, then up an octave to middle C, then back to the center octave, all on one breath.

2. Take a breath and repeat a figure eight pattern on Resonant Hums on one breath, with a strong "mmmmm" sensation on the lips.

3. Take a breath and repeat a figure eight pattern while Gargling Tone on one breath.

4. Take another deep breath, and then perform a Falsetto Slide on a "yah" on the figure eight pattern, sliding down from the center, back to center, up an octave, and back to center. Once you return to center while still maintaining a falsetto tone on the same breath, begin Transcending Tone from falsetto to full voice. Once you've fully transcended to full voice, perform a Siren, first sliding down, then back to center, up an octave, and back to center on the figure eight. All three of the Isolation exercises MUST be performed together on one breath.

All four steps complete one round of the Ultimate Isolation Exercise. There are four basic patterns used to cover this exercise, which will allow you to work the Isolation exercises both up and down, soft and loud, from falsetto to full voice, as well as from full voice to falsetto. The patterns are as follows:

1. <u>Down/Soft</u>—Sliding down first on a dynamically soft volume
2. <u>Down/Loud</u>—Sliding down first on a dynamically loud volume
3. <u>Up/Soft</u>—Sliding up first on a dynamically soft volume
4. <u>Up/Loud</u>—Sliding up first on a dynamically loud volume

By incorporating dynamics, you exhaust the vocal muscles, resulting in quicker gains in muscle and range. Listen to the Ultimate Isolation Exercise Guides listed at the end of this chapter, and by the end of the day you'll understand my madness. By tomorrow you'll understand the simplicity of this exercise, but you will also know that this exercise will serve your voice for your lifetime.

To get the best out of your voice during this exercise, ALWAYS start as low as you can, ALWAYS working upscale first. There are two ways to perform this exercise, each combining two of the four basic patterns, based on two dynamics, loud and soft. Once you've reached the highest note, switch the figure eight pattern as follows:

Dynamically Soft
1. Working upscale=Slide down/Soft volume
2. Working downscale=Slide up/Soft volume

Note: For the dynamically soft approach, once you finish the Lip Bubbles, Resonant Hums, and Gargling Tone, you would perform, in order, Falsetto Slides, Transcending Tones from falsetto to full voice, ending with Sirens. Slide down first on Falsetto Slides and Sirens when working upscale. Slide up first on Falsetto Slides and Sirens when working downscale.

Dynamically Loud
3. Working upscale=Slide down/Loud volume
4. Working downscale=Slide up/Loud volume

Note: For the dynamically loud approach, once you finish the Lip Bubbles, Resonant Hums, and Gargling Tone, you would perform, in order, Sirens, Transcending Tones from full voice to falsetto, ending with Falsetto Slides. Slide down first on Sirens and Falsetto Slides when working upscale. Slide up first on Sirens and Falsetto Slides when working downscale.

There are other patterns you can create for the figure eight, such as changing the dynamic as opposed to sliding direction, but I prefer that you don't switch the dynamic (soft/loud) during your practice session. It won't hurt you, but I've found by maintaining the dynamic and only switching the direction of the slide, you'll achieve the best results.

When I first started practicing this exercise, I alternated between dynamically soft and loud every other week, working Monday through Friday, each day changing the vowel as follows:

Monday—"Ah" as in "Father"
Tuesday—"A" as in "Play"
Wednesday—"E" as in "Sweet"
Thursday—"Oh" as in "Toe"
Friday—"Oo" as in "Food"

Once you've grown accustomed to this exercise, you can use all five vowels for each pitch per day. In other words, perform Lip Bubbles, Resonant Hums, and Gargling Tone, then repeat all three Isolation exercises five times in a row, working each vowel through all three Isolation exercises before moving up or down a half step in range. When working all five vowels, it will take approximately one minute to perform the exercise per each pitch.

It's crucial that you assume the correct facial expressions for each vowel; the following pictures will guide you:

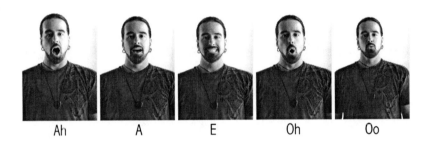

Ah A E Oh Oo

When forming each vowel, ALWAYS keep the tip of the tongue against the back of the bottom teeth, while maintaining a slight yawning sensation to keep the tongue down, forming each vowel as follows:

- ALWAYS begin each vowel with a "Y" consonant.
- When forming "Yah" drop the jaw on a yawn.
- When forming "Yay" think "Yah" with a smile.
- When forming "Yee" smile with touching teeth.
- When forming "Yoh", drop the jaw and think the "Dr. Evil" voice.
- When forming "You" pretend to close the lips around a straw.
- NEVER allow the vowel shape to change when performing the exercise!

Before moving on, I want to offer several basic tips to help you get the most out of the Ultimate Isolation exercise:

Useful Tip: Mastering Transcending Tone

I know, I know, the T.T. exercise is a tough cookie to crumble. For those still struggling with the Transcending Tone exercise, pretend you have a round, deflated balloon in your mouth. The balloon is completely empty on falsetto, but as you swell to full voice, the balloon begins to expand. Once you reach full voice, the balloon is fully expanded and you should feel the soft sensation of the balloon pressing against the roof of your mouth, as well as pressing down against your tongue to keep it from buckling up. This visualization tends to keep students from cracking as they swell from falsetto to full voice and allows for a smooth transition.

Another way to master this exercise is by practicing the Transcending Tone exercise while performing Lip Bubbles. This allows you to transcend from falsetto to full voice without focusing on the vowel, which allows you to focus on pure vocal cord function, as James Lugo, author of *James Lugo's Vocal Insanity*, would put it. In other words, by eliminating the vowel and focusing on Lip Bubbles, the vocal cords can focus purely on creating that seal. **Transcending Tones on Lip Bubbles**

Now that you've locked in on Transcending Tone, it should be noted that when transcending at low pitches on the Ultimate Isolation Exercise, it may feel as if the tone is not falsetto but a very soft full voice tone. You would be correct, which is why it helps to focus on the soft dynamic and start the low "falsetto" as soft as dynamically possible for the Falsetto Slides and Transcending Tones. Don't stress over whether you are in falsetto or full voice. Only focus on the sound being as tiny and clear as possible

Useful Tip: Mastering Gargling Tone

You cannot skip the Gargling Tone exercise during the Ultimate Isolation Exercise. If it's still difficult for you to perform, use water to produce the gargling sound. Over several weeks, cut down the amount of water until you don't need the crutch anymore. **Mastering Gargling Tone**

Now let's get back to the exercise. I've got several key points that will help you master this simple beast. First, it should be noted that this exercise can dry out the voice. Therefore, I recommend you drink a minimum of twenty ounces of water per every fifteen minutes of your workout session. You'll need lots of water for this exercise to keep the cords hydrated.

Next, as you perform the Lip Bubbles, Resonant Hums, and Gargling Tone, "think" the exact vowel you are using during the Isolation half of the exercise. For example, if you are using the "Oh" vowel, mentally think that you are forming the "Oh" vowel on Lip Bubbles, Resonant Hums, and shape the mouth to the correct

"Oh" vowel position on Gargling Tone. It helps to shape the mouth correctly for muscle memory. This only applies if you are performing the exercise while working one vowel. If you are using all vowels per pitch, this tip does not apply. Now let's get back to the exercise.

Last, it is EXTREMELY important that you maintain your softest and loudest voice during this exercise. When **Vocalizing Dynamically Soft**, it must be so tiny in volume and pure in tone that it sounds as if a fly were singing. NO breathiness! The exact amount of breath pressure you should be experiencing on soft volume equals the least amount of breath you'd need to get the vocal cords vibrating. When **Vocalizing Dynamically Loud**, it needs to be as loud as possible WITHOUT sounding as if you are shouting or straining. Remember Rocky Balboa from *Raise Your Voice.* Loud will NOT hurt your voice. It will only hurt your voice if you do not support.

When singing soft or loud, do NOT change the volume level except for when you are Transcending Tone! When Transcending Tone, the dynamic should transcend as smoothly as the tone. When in soft voice, do not raise the volume—even a decibel—as you slide up or down. The same rules apply to the dynamically loud voice. Don't make the voice louder to hit the higher notes, or let your loud voice diminish in volume. Always maintain the dynamic.

USING THE CIRCLE

Now that we've discussed the Ultimate Isolation Exercise in its true form, I would like to add that there is nothing wrong with using the circle as opposed to the figure eight. In some instances it may be more beneficial. If you are only able to cover three to four notes using the figure eight pattern, use the circle until your voice has grown to three octaves to ensure you get plenty of practice time. Once you have a solid three-octave range, you will be able to practice daily, covering a full octave with the figure eight.

Circles are also useful for those who wish to work the Transcending Tone on higher notes, as many singers have expressed their concern with only working the Transcending Tone exercise in their lower range when performing the Ultimate Isolation Exercise. I assure you, even in the low range, you are benefiting from the exercise. However, use the circle if you feel the need.

You can also work the individual Isolation exercises over a weak area in your range that you wish to strengthen. But I suggest using the individual exercises after the Ultimate Isolation Exercise, applying the circle approach when doing so.

That's the Ultimate Isolation Exercise in a nutshell. Take your time and reread this chapter, studying each audio example. Don't get aggravated. It'll click soon enough and then you can use it as your secret weapon. If you need more guidance, I cover this exercise in the second year of Vendera Vocal Academy, teach it in private and

Skype lessons, and demonstrate it in my *Beyond Vocal Strength Training* video from BeyondtheVoice.com. Trust me, the Ultimate Isolation exercise works! Listen to the following audio guides and you'll be a pro in no time:

Ultimate Isolation Guide (Figure Eight) Soft Dynamic
Ultimate Isolation Guide (Figure Eight) Loud Dynamic
Ultimate Isolation Guide (Circle) Soft Dynamic
Ultimate Isolation Guide (Circle) Loud Dynamic

Useful Tip: Don't Crack in the Back

I want to share one of my favorite sayings, which is "If I leave it in the back I'm going to crack." This phrase refers to your placement on Lip Bubbles, Resonant Hums, and the "E" and "Oo" vowels. If you don't feel that vibration against your teeth and the hard palate ridge on these particular exercises/vowels, your voice will crack. So, when a student cracks, I repeat this phrase, they change their focus of placement and they discover they can go higher without cracking by moving the buzz to the front, and not leaving it in the back. So, if this happens to you, just remember, "If I leave it in the back, I am going to crack."

Useful Tip: Using a Straw to Master Isolation Exercises

As a final tip, I like to say that you must be comfortable with the six exercises that comprise the Ultimate Isolation exercise stack. If you're having trouble maintaining any of the warm ups (Lip Bubbles, Resonant Hums, Gargling Tone) or the three Isolation exercises (Falsetto Slide, Transcending Tone, Siren) without cracking, then a straw might be the answer. Stick a straw into a bottle half filled with water and practice sliding or transcending on different pitches. Using a straw in water will put a cap on the amount of air you can release because the water bubbles will slow the release. In turn, the resonance of your pitch will float back up the straw and down your throat actually massaging your vocal cords with sound. You'll notice that the exercises seem to be much easier to perform in the manner, with less cracking, and a more even tone and volume. This is very therapeutic for the vocal cords and very effective for enhanced training and mastery of these exercises. Feel free to spend a few weeks performing all six exercises separately via the straw and water before moving on to the Ultimate Isolation exercise. Remember, this is NOT a race, so get the exercises right first before attacking the advanced routine.

Now, let's revisit our rock roots.

REVISITING FOR HARD ROCKERS ONLY

SINGING HARD ROCK IS AN ART FORM, and one that can be done safely. I know firsthand. When a team of doctors tested my voice for loudness and examined my vocal cords with a camera, they were surprised when I sustained a soprano A# multiple times at over 120 decibels and more surprised by the fact that my vocal cords showed no signs of wear and tear after years of screaming and breaking glass with my voice. When I demonstrated AC/DC and Alice in Chains-type grit as they viewed my vocal cords on a monitor, they were even more surprised that I could scream effortlessly without any strain or compression in the pharynx above the vocal cords. FYI—screaming and grit use the same techniques as clean singing, which is why it can be done safely.

In all honesty, I'm not too concerned with the physical aspects of how grit is achieved, though I speculate it's because the vocal cords are compressing a bit tighter as well as slight manipulation by the false folds and pharynx. When we've viewed my vocal cords via scope, we actually noticed compression in the cords allowing two spots to vibrate along the edges of the actual vocal cords with the false folds only intervening on certain types of grit by adding a sound effect much like clapping the hands together (no actual pitch created, just a flapping, slapping sound added to the regular grit). But in the end, who cares? Knowing HOW it occurs internally will NOT make you a better screamer. If I understood which muscles caused me to vomit, it wouldn't prevent me from hurling the next time I got food poisoning.

So, PLEASE don't get caught up in this latest craze of trying to scientifically break down singing by understanding the cricothyroid. It's not going to make you a better singer. What will make you a better singer, and better screamer is lots of practice via vocal exercises using correct vocal technique, followed by singing your butt off. Speaking of practice, I've decided to throw in some bonus exercises for you hard rockers.

THE GRIT SIREN

I introduced this exercise in *Extreme Scream Volume 2*. But I figured I'd elaborate with some more audio guidance. Basically, it's a gritty version of the Siren. It should be done in moderation and you should stop the exercise if it makes you cough or if it hurts your throat. You must have an understanding of how grit is produced as explained in the *Extreme Scream* series and *Raise Your Voice* before attempting this exercise. Listen to the **Grit Siren** exercise before giving it a try.

STAIR STEPPING YOUR EXERCISES

Stair stepping is a unique way to walk up and down the scale one pitch at a time. It would be the equivalent of standing at the bottom of a set of stairs, walking up one step, returning to the bottom, walking up two steps, returning to the bottom, up three, back down, and so forth. The E-Scream is perfect for stair stepping.

I'm always performing the basic E-Scream while stair stepping to cover my glass-breaking notes. I start on tenor C with a goal of working up to a soprano G to cover all the pitches of the wine glasses that I break. I stair-step the E-Scream as follows:

C-C#-C-C#-D-C#-C-C#-D-D#-D-C#-C-C#-D-D#-E-D#-D-C#-C-C#-D-
D#-E-F-E-D#-D-C#-C-C#-D-D#-E-F-F#-F-E-D#-D-C#-C-C#-D-D#-E-F-
F#-G-F#-F-E-D#-D-C#-C

Stair stepping from tenor C to soprano G results in fifty-seven E-Screams as opposed to eight when using the conventional scale. **E-Scream Stair Stepping Example** This approach allows you to isolate a smaller section of notes, working each note repeatedly to build more muscle in the area of those adducted pitches.

It's a useful approach for working through tough areas and can be used for any exercise. For example, if you can only work the Ultimate Isolation Exercise up to a G above middle C and cannot reach that G#. The easiest way to reach that elusive G# is to drop four notes from your top note, in this case, down to an E, and begin stair stepping. You would perform the Ultimate Isolation Exercise on each note as follows:

E-F-E-F-F#-F-E-F-F#-G-F#-F-E-F-F#-G-G#-G-F#-F-E

That elusive G# should finally come to you. If not, keep working; a few days of stair stepping will get you there! Use stair stepping anytime you need to build muscle in an area of the range that is troubling you.

E-SCREAM SIREN

Here's another cool exercise that can be performed regularly or stair-stepped. Building on the E-Scream, perform a reverse Siren after swelling to your loud, reinforced falsetto, sliding down one octave, and then sliding back up an octave to your original note, finishing by transcending the loud reinforced E-Scream falsetto back into a light falsetto. If it helps, think of the circle as you slide. **E-Scream Siren**

It should be noted that a slight muscle ache may occur from these exercises, especially when stair stepping. This is normal and is caused by muscle fatigue. If your throat feels tired or sore, stop the exercises for the day. If your voice begins to feel scratchy, stop altogether, because you might be straining. As the muscles gain strength, you'll develop more vocal stamina and these sensations will dissipate.

You may also notice dizziness on the high notes. That is normal as well, though our goal is for that sensation to eventually pass. If dizziness is accompanied by a headache, it's a sign that the loud notes are being produced by pushing too much air by shouting. Your loud tone should occur as a result of total support and resonance production. Bottom line, a headache is not a good sign.

Years ago, during the writing of *Raise Your Voice* when I was playing in a bar band with my buddies Tim Odle, Greg Seymour, and Joe Conley, I had a migraine after one particular gig. It was due to over-pushing to compensate for the pain in my neck muscles. I was recovering from neck surgery and I was struggling to sing freely. I went against my own technique philosophy and blasted out the notes.

By the end of that night, my migraine was so severe that I could barely see straight. I then knew I needed to get my act together before I caused irreparable damage. Follow my example. If you develop a migraine, stop singing immediately. You are using too much breath to release your notes.

Useful Tip: Changing Your Point of Reference
If you feel your range has plateaued with nowhere to go, move your beginning point of reference four or five notes higher. Here are three standard point-of-reference changes I use based on vocal "breaks" for all singers, both male and female:

Original Point of Reference	New Point of Reference
C	F
F	A
A	D

By raising your point of reference, you are skipping the lows, pressing into the highs much sooner in the exercise. Your voice and mind are used to starting the exercise lower in pitch. This is a way of mentally tricking the voice and mind into thinking you are singing lower. When you reach those troubling breaks or high notes, the voice and mind will expect to work through them easily, thinking they are lower in pitch. This is not cheating; it's simply a way of getting the subconscious out of your way and allowing you to nail those notes that you already own.

Anyone who has had a lesson with me will tell you how I love to fib about the notes they are sustaining. For example, if I fib to a student who has trouble hitting a tenor C by telling them the tenor C is an A#, nine times out of ten I can have that student several notes above tenor C without much effort. However, when I tell them we're going for the tenor C (when it's actually a D# or E), that is the point where they usually begin to strain because their mindset, which says that tenor C is their troubled note, prevents them from going higher. When they realize they are actually several notes above tenor C, it blows their mind.

You CAN reach those elusive, seemingly unreachable pitches. It simply takes lots of practice and changing your mindset when it comes to thinking about high notes. There you have it, hard rock at its best. Now, let's revisit the stage and studio.

REVISITING THE STAGE & STUDIO

Y OU CAN NEVER LEARN ENOUGH about your craft. So let's discuss more stage and studio tips to help you achieve the next level.

REVISITING THE STAGE

You are what you think. Therefore, to be a singing superstar you need to adjust your thoughts. Case in point, the ability to channel our nervous energy to fuel our performance is heavily dictated by our mindset. Luckily, we have hypnosis expert Matt Adams (aka Max Action), creator of the *Vocal Mindset* series, to help us master our mindset. I trust in Matt's guidance so much that a few years ago Matt created a "Glass Shattering Mindset" program just for me, which I've used for shows all around the world. He has since created a new approach that goes beyond *Vocal Mindset I & II*, called *Vocal Mindset 3D*. Here's Matt to explain how to tap into the three-dimensional vocal mindset to help you think and perform like a superstar.

THE SECRET TO BECOMING A MUSIC LEGEND
By Matt Adams
If you've ever wanted to become an amazing singer that people know and love, there's an unspoken industry secret that you must know.

There's a global myth in the music industry that says the most talented people will become the megastars. Most singers <u>think</u> all they need is their talent, and yet there are hundreds of thousands of musicians that still don't and will never get the recognition they deserve.

And likewise, I'm sure you've seen singers that you wonder how they got as famous as they are because they kinda … well … suck. Talent, while important, won't get you the success you want on its own. Here's why:

You've already got talent, and what Jaime is teaching you will give you that sharpened edge that will put you ahead of 90 percent of other singers out there vocally. However, if you want a chance to survive, you must look at what professional singers that have already made it did to get to where they are today.

Whether you want to be a superstar recording artist performing for millions of people or you just want to sing better as a hobby, I'm about to give you the game changer you'll need to do it.

The real secret to their success wasn't just their talent, but their ability to use their mind and imagine what they want and make it into a reality. In other words, it was their MINDSET.

Your mindset is what's going to get you to do the overwhelming amount of stuff it's going to take to get you to the superstardom you dream about and really maximize your potential as a singer. The singer with the greatest potential in the world will never become a superstar if they can't direct their mind to do what's necessary for that success.

Now, some artists are able to create a smash hit before fading back into the darkness from whence they came, and others are able to create a long-running career with multiple smash hits. We're going to focus on the mindset of the artists who can create the multiple smash hits.

Lack of mindset is the single biggest cause of failure

Remember that no amount of talent will bring you that long-standing success you're looking for if you don't have the mindset to keep it on track; not lack of talent, as most people would believe.

So here's a question for you: If I showed you the four key components to an unstoppable mindset that would create the exact level of success you want, whether it's performing for millions of people or just getting wicked good, could you do it?

I bet you could. And I know your mindset will be the single most important cause of your success or failure as a singer. Jaime has given you the tools; now he's entrusted me to show you how to get yourself to use them for maximum effectiveness.

Your mind directs your actions, and your actions create your success. If you don't build the mindset of a superstar within yourself, you'll struggle and become frustrated, and you won't see the success you're looking for.

So, are you ready to kick your career into high gear? Here are the four keys:

Key #1—POWER

This is the first step to capturing your dream and enjoying the ride. Since your mind directs your actions, and your actions create your success, our first target is showing you how to control thoughts and emotions.

This is what gives you the power to control what you do and when you do it, like getting over fear of the stage, or a tendency to procrastinate when it's time to practice, or the mental creative blocks you might experience. I want you to tap your true power and potential as a singer and artist.

Until we can know and control ourselves, we'll never be able to control our destiny. Here's an example. Have you ever known someone that's a procrastinator? No matter what, they would put things off until the last minute or even miss their opportunity because they hesitated.

For whatever reason, whether it was fear, anxiety, or they just didn't feel like doing it, something important didn't get done and they're still sitting in the same place they were before.

This happens to all of us at one point or another; we don't feel like doing something so we'll find any other distraction we can. The reality is that this quickly becomes an ugly pattern that if we don't know how to control it, we'll never be in control of our success.

I'm as guilty of this as anyone, if not more so. I wasted several years of my life just because I didn't know how my mind worked and I couldn't get myself to do what I knew I needed to do in order to become successful. Once I figured it out, it was like an explosion of potential and excitement and success.

When I started working with singers on their mindset, I found that most of them were only focused on singing techniques, which is great at the beginning. But it's like turning on a fire hose full blast with no one holding it. It's spewing power everywhere and there's no control over the flow, which creates more destruction than achieving a goal.

There are also many negative pitfalls that attract and destroy the lives and careers of unsuspecting singers that don't know how to control their thoughts and emotions, such as drugs, alcohol, partying, and the other nonsense that comes along with becoming the star everyone loves (think Amy Winehouse).

I'll say it again. If you don't have the power to control your thoughts and emotions, then you won't have the power to control where your career goes. The good news is that you can and should be learning how your mind works and how to control it.

I knew a guy out here in Los Angeles that had an amazing voice, and his talent drew people in, including music producers from big record labels. There was one problem, though. This guy just couldn't seem to control himself. He would show up late to meetings, flip out if things weren't going his way, and let's just say he had some habits that weren't helping him keep his head on straight. When I asked what had got him all twisted, he shook his head and just looked at me with that look of helplessness in his eyes and said, "I don't know. I just do it."

The guy had talent that got people's attention, but his lack of control over his thoughts and emotions pushed them away. He was, in one word, powerless.

Your power comes from your ability to create and condition good habits, feelings, and beliefs that get you what you want and eliminate the bad ones that hold you back. Beliefs and habits like:

- Being completely confident in your abilities
- Loving to practice every day
- Pushing yourself to be better
- Knowing you're worthy of the fame you desire
- Being able to change your mood from fear to power, or anger to determination in an instant
- Staying hungry for success and always pushing to the next level
- Conditioning your mind to take action NOW. This component of power reminds me of when I was trying to cook with an oven that would sometimes heat to the correct temperature but sometimes heat too high or too low. There was no consistency, and I was <u>powerless</u> to stop it.

The difference in temperature meant the food was either burnt or undercooked; one tasted horrible and the other could get you sick. I had no consistency, because I couldn't control the temperature of the oven. But I still had one chance. I got a new oven. Buying a new oven was something I could do to change my results, and from then on I've had direct control over the temperature, and everything has always turned out exactly as I want it.

You've got the power to change your life by taking control of your thoughts and emotions and building that control into your mindset. Choose to think positively, plain and simple.

Key #2—CLARITY

Once you're empowered, it's time to know where you want to go. Having a clearly defined vision of what you want your career to be will put you ahead of 99 percent of singers, because most singers don't know what they want other than they want to sing. The more narrowly you define what you want and who you want to become, the better chance you have of getting it.

Realize that as an artist you've got to have an identity that's larger than life if you want your music and voice to move people. Your public wants to get to know you and relate to you through your music, your personality, your lyrics, and it's hard to do that if even you don't know who you are.

One of the laws of the subconscious mind that I teach is, "A confused mind will never take action." It's like a deer caught in the headlights. If you don't know what you want, it's hard to start doing anything.

Here are some questions to get you started. Answer them as best you can and continue to refine them. Remember, the more you know about you and what you want, the better your chances of getting it.

- What type of music would you love to sing most?
- How big would you like your career to be? (Be specific, not, "I don't care" or "Really big." What does "Really big" look like?) Sold-out arenas, multi-platinum albums, agents, publicists, etc.
- Who is already doing what you'd like to do? Make sure you're not trying to be the next insert famous singer here. This is a career killer because you'll just look and sound like a copycat.
- What are you willing to do to achieve your dream? Before you say "ANYTHING," think about your answer. Are you willing to miss time with your family, put in hours of practice, hustle, and knock on doors? This is important, and you'll see why in the next component.
- What checkpoints do you have for yourself?
- What can you do right now to put your career on the right track?
- Who do you know that can help you and who can you get contact info for and introduce yourself to? Remember becoming powerful and getting over your fear. Call someone up, introduce yourself, let them know you're going to be a star. Then keep in contact.

Distractions are the most prevalent thing in our lives today. Email, cell phones, work, social media, bills, TV, etc. Each of these distractions can pull you away from your dream. If you're not crystal clear on your dreams and don't have the power to control your thoughts and emotions, it's easier to become distracted.

I was watching the show *The Voice*, and there was some guy on there that had an extremely amazing voice. He was showcased because he could sing, rap, do opera; the guy could basically do it all. And guess how many chairs turned around? **NONE.**

No one could argue that the guy didn't have talent, but unfortunately no one could figure out where to use his talent. Because of everything he could do, the coaches had to make multiple decisions on the fly about who they saw him as. It was too confusing. As we've said before, confusion creates inaction.

It was his job to tell the coaches who he was with his talent, but he tried to be everything to everyone and just confused the coaches.

You don't want your fans having to decide what or who you are; you want to be crystal clear on it before that. When you're clear on who you are, what you're about, and what your sound is, that's when you give your audience a chance to identify with you. That's when they want to know your story, and that's when you become a star.

Key #3—STRATEGY

Now that you've got control of getting yourself to do what's necessary, and you have clarity on knowing what to do, it's time to develop the strategy for getting there.

A better strategy will overcome better talent any day. This is the secret weapon that allows the unknown singer to get their big break, because everyone else is still thinking talent is what determines who wins.

Here's an example of strategy in action. If I have a can of tuna that I want to open, I can try to open it with brute force by smashing it with a rock, or I can use a better strategy and use a can opener. Both ways will work, but using an open mindset and strategy gives much faster, cleaner, and reliable results.

From a long time of coaching and speaking, I've seen many people that have attended motivational and business seminars that left empowered and were ready to take on the world with nothing but a "Can Do" attitude. A "Can Do" attitude is great, but on its own it can lead to more failures because these people think anything and everything they do is going to work.

There's no clarity, just a big picture and the attitude that they can't fail. This obviously isn't reality.

It's going to be different for you because you're getting the empowerment, and then you're taking the smart route by getting crystal clear on what you want and who you want to become.

The reason I want you to be crystal clear about your outcome is that now we can use it to build a strategy of getting exactly that. Remember, this is your life and career. It should be as fulfilling and exciting as you want it to be. The strategy we use is going to be of extreme importance, and here's why:

The music industry is difficult enough as it is, so you don't want to compete blindly; you want to compete strategically. Once again, it's easy to think you're just competing on talent, but you're not. You're competing on showmanship, sound, marketing, and sheer will to succeed.

What is it that you do that completely separates you from everyone else? In a now cluttered world of music it's crucial that you have a strategy to rise above all the noise. What can you do to separate yourself from all the other options out there?

Take Lady Gaga for instance. Whether you like her music or not, you've got to admit she sure does put on a show. That's been her strategy for getting to the top. It's the same with metal bands like Rammstein and Slipknot. Michael Jackson was an amazing singer and performer who brought his music to life, and his fans adored him for it. Willie Nelson and The Beatles still have huge followings not just because of their talents, but because of their performance and sound. (And all of your favorite artists are also in this category.)

So, in order to create the best strategy, we've got to go back to your crystal clear vision:

- Who is your demographic? (What age range?)
- How can you get in front of these people? (What are they watching or participating in?)
- Who can get you in front of these people?
- Who are they already listening to and what can they identify with?

This is part of your mindset—becoming the performer you want to be. Knowing and loving your audience and being exactly what they're looking for.

Justin Beiber has become a MEGA STAR because his audience is little girls that think he's cute and want to be his girlfriend. They buy all his posters and music and T-shirts. We want you to have that kind of effect on your audience.

- What is it you stand for?
- What's your story?
- What are your beliefs and values?
- What kind of story do you want to tell with your voice?
- What's your sound that's real to you?

All of this MUST become your mindset. These answers will start showing through your voice and your performance, and these answers are key to building a real strategy that has the potential to rocket you to the greatest achievements of your career.

I don't want you to just be inspired; I want you to build this amazing mindset that will get you the results and career you dream about. Your music and your voice can and will inspire millions of people, change their moods, and leave them always wanting more. Now let's begin building this mindset.

Key #4—CONDITIONS

Conditions can be best understood by looking at reality.

Let's say you want to plant a flower. What would you need? You'd need seeds, dirt, water, and sunlight.

Without these four things you'll never see any growth. Why? Because the conditions aren't there. Your flower won't grow in a steel box in the back of a cave because the conditions won't allow it. It also won't grow in the ice fields of Antarctica, because it's too cold.

But put that seed in some dirt, give it a little water and some sunlight, and you've got growth in days and beautiful blooms within weeks. In other words, you can progress faster than you ever imagined when the conditions are right. Here are the conditions to become a superstar singer:

- Practice solid vocal technique, which Jaime has given you.
- Take care of your voice.
- Surround yourself with people that can help you in your career. Call them up even if they don't live in the same state, and introduce yourself.
- Make demos of your songs or music videos. Who cares about the quality at first, the point is you're doing something.
- Do you have people that support you or laugh at your dream? Supporters can stay; the rest will only hold you back.
- How many gigs are you booking for yourself each week?

Are you starting to see these conditions I'm talking about? When people ask, "How long is it going to take for me to be successful?" My answer is always, "How long do you want it to take?" The more action you take the quicker your results.

The people you hear on the radio today and see on TV took action. They had a love of music and a vision of being much bigger than just someone singing in the shower. They went and found the people who could and would give them a shot, and the rest is history.

Realize that people in the entertainment business want to work with artists who hustle, have the mindset, and are willing to put in the work. It's all shown by your actions.

Remember, part of your POWER component is conditioning your mind to be ferocious and focused on your dream. Make your dream bigger than you and never wait for someone to come by and give you a chance. You've got to stop them and make them listen. That's the action mindset. For those that don't have this action mindset, they'll be the dreamers that never did.

Your dream won't come to you; you've got to go out and hunt it down. Build your mindset and this will be the adventure of a lifetime, and you can and will become legendary.

In each of these steps there's going to be some resistance to change. It's nothing to be alarmed about; it's just reality, so we'll deal with it.

POWER—An obstacle that's common when stepping into your power is the belief system you already have for yourself. Some musicians have a limitation, thinking that "I'm not good enough" or "I really wish I could sing like _____."

Becoming amazing takes practice, just like anything else. Realize that it's your art, your craft, which means not pushing yourself to sound like someone else but pushing yourself to sound more like you, a better-practiced and improved version of you.

CLARITY—When becoming clear about what you want and who you want to become, make sure you're as specific as possible. Use words that can be measured, such as selling 20,000 downloads in ten hours. This gives you specific numbers to create a strategy for.

Phrases like "Being the best singer in the world" or "Being the best I can be" are very abstract and lead to the question, "How will you know when this happens?"

STRATEGY—Be open to different strategies you may have never thought of. The key to creating a working strategy is to see the world as it actually is currently and not as you think it could or should be.

An example would be someone thinking, "I can get an agent easy because I have an amazing voice." The belief is that having a great voice is all that's necessary to get an agent's attention.

The reality is that an agent hears great voices all the time. We need to realize this and think, "What is it about me that makes me different and more exciting than everyone else this agent will hear?"

CONDITIONS—Change your current conditions to make the environment suitable for the type of career you want. For example, if you want to be a superstar recording artist, seek out and meet people that can help you. You're not going to meet them sitting on the couch or working a 9 to 5 job. This can be one of the hardest things to overcome, because many people want to have an amazing amount of success without changing what they're already doing.

Remember that doing more of what you're already doing will get you more of what you already have. In order for things to change, you must change.

What to Do Right Now

Obviously, I've got a very limited space in this article, and I've got more training for you that's going to amp your mindset and have you getting results that you may have never thought possible.

These free trainings are offered to you as a gift on behalf of Jaime Vendera and the *Raise Your Voice* team. You can get these free training videos by going to http://www.maxactionnow.com.

Copyright © 2012 by Matt Adams. All Rights Reserved. Reprinted with permission.

Matt Adams, aka Max Action, is quickly becoming America's peak-performance expert, showing people how to program their own mind to take massive action, give their best performance every time, and have a better than great chance at success. Max Action's philosophy is, "It doesn't matter how skilled you are if you don't take time to build an unstoppable mindset. With the correct mindset, you can know how to do something and still not do it." Max has coached and inspired over 60,000 people to start action in their lives and has given them the tools to do it consistently. When you program your mind to be excited to do the things that once frustrated you, you become more fulfilled than you've ever felt and get better results. Max Action currently offers free mindset training at his website MaxActionNow.com.

Useful Tip: I Am That … Because I Said So!

Many of my lessons revolve around instilling a positive mindset in the student. I repeatedly hear stories of how a singer doesn't believe in himself or herself. Even during vocal exercises, I catch singers shaking their heads at their performance. Carrying a negative thought pattern about yourself and your performance is guaranteed to bring down your sense of self worth. Therefore, I tell all my students to think about what they want to be as a singer, and then add "I am that" before the sentence, and "because I said so" at the end of the sentence. If a singer says, "I want to be an amazing soul singer," I have them change it to, "I am that amazing soul singer, because I said so!" "I am that" allows you to look at yourself or the situation from a third-person point of view. If you just said, "I am an amazing soul singer," you are examining yourself. But when you add "that" it's as if you can look at yourself objectively. "Because I said so" allows you to own that statement. It's like commanding the subconscious to get in line with your rules. So, when you're feeling down, think about what you want and then realize that "you are that." Repeat it throughout the day to reinforce the statement.

Now let's move from mindset to stage performance tips. First things first; you MUST know your songs. There's nothing worse than forgetting lyrics. Singers who tend to forget lyrics have asked me how to beat this problem. First, I have them print out the lyrics, then handwrite the lyrics onto a separate sheet, and finally sing the song three times in a row, using their finger to trace each word on the handwritten page as they sing. The "writing down and tracing the words as you sing" method embeds the song into the mind. From there I expect my students to sing every day, utilizing soft singing to master the song.

When singing cover tunes you don't want to be a parrot (as I mentioned in *RYV*). However, you do want to represent the singer well when you do cover another singer's repertoire. A friend of mine, vocal coach/singer Eli Prinsen of The Sacrificed, was asked to record with the band Sacred Warrior, so I asked him how he approached singing the band's previous material without being a parrot, while respecting the original singer's style. Here's what he had to say:

SINGING ANOTHER SINGER'S SONGS
By Eli Prinsen
Joining a band with an established sound and fan base can be difficult, especially if the band is taking things into a new direction. You have the responsibility of pulling off singing the well-known previous material as well as offering up your own vocals to create the new sound of the band.

During the audition process for Sacred Warrior, I was asked to do both. I sang two new songs from the album as well as one of their well-known songs. Their selecting this song was to see if I could sing the previous material and have the ability to sing in that mid–high range for extended periods of time.

This is when all of your hard work and dedication in vocal training pays off and gives you the confidence, ability, and excitement to meet the challenge.

I have my own approach for covering an especially tough song and preparing myself mentally and physically for the vocal stamina and range stamina that the song requires, and I'd like to share it with you all. I'll tell you what I do, and then why I do it.

First, I listen to the lyrics very carefully, paying attention to the vowels, being aware of any explosive consonants. For each singer there is usually a certain vowel that for some reason comes more easily to the singer, and they may tend to write toward that vowel, or express that vowel, even clinging to that vowel when singing other vowels. An example of this would be singing a line like "pictures of our dreams." Instead of pronouncing "dreams" with an E sound, the singer pronounces it more with an A sound, like "pictures of our drames." Another example of this would be "children of the damned" being pronounced "children of the deemed," with the singer clinging more toward an E vowel, probably a vowel he sings with more confidence. So pay attention to this and address it if this gives a "signature sound" to the song. If you feel you need to replicate these vowels, then do so by doing vowel modification slides that stretch the vowels in an even, controlled manner. The following exercise will help you to sing various words in your higher range more easily, and it comes in handy when used for the application listed above.

Vowel Modification Slide—Singing an Ah, then sliding up an octave and transitioning the Ah toward an Uh once it reaches the top of the octave, then sliding down from the Uh back to the Ah at the bottom of the octave. And so on and so forth with all of the vowels: Ah to Uh, A to Eh, Oh to AW, Ooh to Uh, Oh to Aw.

Second, listen for glottal shocks on any of the vowels. Take the damaging attack off of these vowels by adding a very slight "H" to the beginning of the vowel and you will reduce the wear and tear on your vocal cords. An example where glottal shocks may occur is evident in the lyrics, "I'm getting even." The I and the E can create shocks to your cords. Approach the I and the E with a small H sound. Do this with all of your songs, not just covers.

Third, just as you listened to the original singer's vowels, listen to their vibrato. Is it a pulsating vibrato? Is it pitch-to-pitch vibrato? How is the timing of the vibrato? Pay attention and address the issue.

Fourth, listen all around and in between the lyrics for breaks when you can manage your breathing more efficiently. Say that there are a lot of words in each line of the verse and then a small break before the chorus. Obviously, before the long verse you know to take in the appropriate amount of air needed, but effectively utilize that small break to expel any unused air in your lungs and get a few deep cleansing breaths through your nose and out of your mouth and keep the inhalation feeling of the ribcage the entire time you're vocalizing. Also, it is helpful during the guitar solo to do a few swallowing motions (with or without water) and a few quick jaw shakes and neck stretches to keep the muscles feeling loose and limber.

Fifth, remember the power of visualization. Focus on the feeling of the resonance up in the head and out of the throat. Remember the range you are capable of and don't allow yourself to be psyched out by the song. Remind yourself that all of the notes are within your capability, and approach the high notes as if they were comfortable mid notes with a sense of confidence and release, imagining the successful execution of every note before and while you're singing it. This is extremely useful for pitch accuracy as well.

Finally, record yourself singing the song. Listen back with a critical ear. Practice singing it several times throughout the course of the week, rerecord it and you will be shocked at the improvement.

Eli Prinsen is the lead vocalist of U.S. Christian power metal bands Sacred Warrior and The Sacrificed. A vocal enthusiast, Eli has trained with some of the world's most renowned vocal coaches and ultimately founded his own voice training system, the Hybrid Vocal Technique, which he created specifically for the rock, metal, and power metal vocalists for an approach to full-range singing. Learn more at hybridvocaltechnique.com.

STUDYING LIVE PERFORMANCE VIDEOS

Eli had some great points, but it doesn't end with singing; you must also master your moves. If you're going to be a performer you had best get your stage act together. With the evolution of YouTube, you have a vast amount of training tools at your fingertips. I'm referring to live concert performances. Begin studying your favorite singers as they perform on stage. Watch their mannerisms; notice how they use their hands, body, and eyes to connect to the audience. Think of these movements as live performance tricks and begin incorporating them into your own live show. For example, when Marq Torien of the BulletBoys performs, he tends to slither side to side like a cobra. In my younger years, I incorporated a similar move.

When you begin trying new moves, practice in front of a mirror. How does it look? Stupid or cool? Be honest, because you want to wow your audience. By practicing your stage moves in front of a mirror, you can decide whether to keep the move or toss it, whether it's a shake of the hips, the pointing of a hand, or a glare of the eyes. I also suggest that you practice your moves as much as you do your singing. You have to become as comfortable with moving around on stage as you do with singing.

HONING THE CONCERT VOICE

Your stage performance has much to do with how you connect with your audience, but let's not forget your internal voice. Have you ever noticed when you're at a concert singing along with the singer that you can literally feel your voice on the roof of your mouth and it feels as if it's effortless. Generally, it's tough to hear yourself sing at a concert because of all the noise of the crowd combined with loud music.

When you sing at a concert, you must rely on the physical sensation of your voice as opposed to hearing the pitch. You might even recall that the palate buzz seemed stronger during those unbridled moments of singing your brains out, not worrying what the person beside you was thinking.

The concert voice is what we want to maintain at all times, because it will protect our voice and keep us in tune. You can still cup your hand over your ear, use a VAM, rely on floor monitors or in-ears, but the concert voice will keep you in check when all else fails. For me, the concert voice consists of total palate buzz all the way from the back of my throat to the very front, buzzing all my top teeth.

The next time you're at a concert and singing your brains out, pay attention to the physical sensation of the concert voice. Commit it to memory, and then focus on repeating the sensation at all rehearsals and gigs.

Useful Tip: Quit Smiling—Start Smawning

I've repeatedly mentioned in other books and lessons (if you've worked with me) how important it is to add the slight yawn on a micro breath. I'm also sure you'll remember my pushing you to smile when singing, just as Jim Gillette taught me. I like to tell my students to smile and yawn simultaneously—or smawn—throughout their performance. Smawning widens the soft palate, opening the inside of the dome so you can easily feel the buzz on the roof of the mouth, thus taking weight off the voice. So, smawn more often and set your voice free. This one tip is worth its weight in gold. Utilize it every time you sing!

Note: The smawn doesn't apply to the vowel positions during your practice sessions.

It also helps your singing voice by maintaining body posture, which I discussed in *Raise Your Voice* and *Sing Out Loud.* Posture is so important that I asked my good friend Dr. Timothy Jameson to chime in on the subject.

POSTURAL HEALTH & WELLNESS IN THE VOCALIST
By Dr. Timothy Jameson

Excellent vocal technique is dependent upon a complex balance of your muscular systems combined with the health and wellness of your structural systems and internal organs, especially the heart and lungs. Let us evaluate each system and determine its importance to your overall singing ability, and then let's discuss how enhancements can be made to improve your singing.

The health of your structural system is deeply in tune with your posture, i.e., how you position your body while sitting or standing. In addition, *all* previous injuries you have suffered to your musculoskeletal system that have been left untreated by a body worker (chiropractor, massage therapist, Feldenkrais®, or Alexander Technique® instructor) will determine your current level of structural health. Let's examine that further.

If you have been involved in previous moderate to severe injuries, such as a sports trauma, bad falls, car accidents, or severe jarring episodes of your body, you most likely have developed some form of scar tissue formation, ligament deformation, and changes in structural integrity. This is particularly true if you have never had any form of therapy or treatment to help restore balance and alignment. Therefore, vocalists who are attempting to learn and hone their skills with a weakened structural system caused by previous trauma will inherently face more challenges than a person who has little structural weakness. I hope you don't fall into this category, but if you do, don't fret, because help is available to bring wellness to your body! I will talk more about that below.

Even more pervasive in the music industry as a whole, and especially with vocalists, are chronic repetitive traumas and their destructive impact on structural health. Prolonged neck strain due to forward head posture, or "reaching for notes" with your head protruding forward or upward, can lead to muscular micro trauma. These movements can even strain the vocal cords themselves. Vocalists with poor technique will use their neck muscles to attempt to hit notes at the peak of their range, or even within their natural range. This tension pattern can lead to destruction of a singer's vocal cords and constant tension and micro trauma of the spinal muscles and supporting ligaments.

If you watch well-trained vocalists, you will notice complete relaxation of the neck and throat as they sing, along with a natural upright relaxed posture. Their vocal control and intensity come from their abdominals, diaphragm, rib cage, and control of their overall expression of sound using the mouth, tongue, vocal cords, and lips as they sing.

With these major and minor traumas in mind, what does a singer do to improve on their structure while singing? The first step is getting back in control of your posture. Every good voice coach has the vocal student sing in front of a mirror. The purpose is to point out postural tensions as the student sings and to teach methods of relaxation, whether it's in the throat, chest, neck, shoulders, or even pelvis and legs. Reducing tension in your postural muscles while singing affords full vocal expression, maximizes performance, and enhances your tonality.

For this reason, I find that vocalists who care for their bodies through methods that release tension in the muscular and skeletal systems, such as massage therapy or chiropractic care, enjoy a more relaxed posture and can even see improvements in overall vocal control. Investing in your body really has amazing dividends as you consider your career in music, or even if you are enjoying music as an amateur vocalist.

The real tone killer for singers is created by a forward head posture. Many people suffer from this because of the technology age we live in. Constantly sitting at the computer, playing video games, sitting at piano benches hunched over a keyboard, and commuting all create a forward head posture whereby the head sits in front of the body. Normally the ears and shoulders should line up directly in a straight line when you look at the body from the side. Forward head posture is when the ears sit forward of the shoulders, causing the neck to straighten and arch forward. This exerts pressure on the sensitive nerves that control your throat, your neck muscles, and even the glands in your neck. The forward head posture will also tighten the throat and narrow the airways, causing your tone to become less than desirable.

Lastly, the forward head posture exerts tremendous forces on the spinal joints and can even lead to herniated and bulging discs in your neck. If you are young, the good news is that your spine can easily be restored if you tend to carry your head forward. It takes exercise, stretching routines, the help of a chiropractor or physical therapist, and a good vocal coach. The specifics of those methods are outside the scope of this article, but I want to let you know that there is help for you available, and forward head posture can be restored to normal head posture.

For those who are older and have had a forward head posture for years, the outcome may not be as good. There may be permanent spinal changes that will not allow the spine to go completely back to normal. Yet better conditioning, stretching, and exercise, along with chiropractic care, can help your overall posture and bring some wellness back to your structure.

Another area that I find problematic in singers is tension in the rib cage. Many singers hold tremendous tension around the diaphragm muscle (which attaches to your lower rib cage). Any rib cage tension will lead to decreased air intake, as the rib cage expansion is diminished and lung expansion is impacted by this. If you are not taking in air effectively, it impacts your vocal tone and vocal endurance.

Also, rib cage tension impacts your ability to control your breath, which is one of the most important aspects of creating good vocal tone. Rib expansion exercises are great to help discover areas of tension. Simply blowing up balloons can really get you expanding those ribs!

For those singers who have the forward head posture I just talked about, there is almost always a contraction of the upper anterior chest wall due to tension from the anterior neck muscles that attach into the collarbone area. I see this also in asthmatics as they use their upper chest muscles to aid in breathing. As a chiropractor, I frequently must release these muscular tensions in each healing treatment session to help the vocalist breathe deeper and more freely. The impact on tone and vocal endurance is tremendous.

Vocalists are like endurance athletes, except in this particular case the endurance comes from proper breath control, air intake, great technique, and tremendous control and skill. Vocalists must realize that their vocal intensity and endurance is directly proportional to their overall health and wellness.

Aerobic health, fitness level, hydration, nutritional intake, and avoiding bad habits are all part of a vocalist's ability to excel in their craft. Vocalists who are serious about their career must become avid health enthusiasts, seeking to attain a level of muscular, heart, and lung fitness that will allow them to sing for many years without fatigue, as long as they have great vocal technique. Even someone who has great aerobic capacity can have poor vocal technique and wind up with polyps and throat strain. There must be a balance in all areas of wellness for the vocalist to attain and maintain a level of excellence.

In summary, vocalists must consider themselves elite athletes that must care for their bodies and utilize the many methods of health and wellness that are available to them to maximize performance. Great coaching, a health and wellness program, maintaining correct posture, and personal will and goal-setting are all a part of excellence in vocal performance. Go for it.

Dr. Timothy Jameson is a musician, chiropractor, and website and book author. He is the worship pastor at Christ's Community Church in Hayward, Calif., leading on piano, guitar, and vocals. He has been in chiropractic practice for twenty-two years in Castro Valley, Calif. He is the author of two books, Repetitive Strain Injuries *and* Reach For the Top: The Musician's Guide to Health, Wealth, and Success *(Vendera Publishing). He is also the award-winning author of musicianshealth.com. He lives with his wife of 22 years and two teenage children in Hayward, Calif. Dr. Jameson can be reached though* timothyjameson.com *and* jamesonchiro.com.

As a final thought from yours truly, I feel I need to address the issue of a bad performance. Even if you've practiced your butt off, there are times when Murphy's Law kicks in and everything that could possibly go wrong does. When your keyboard quits working, you fall off the stage, or your voice doesn't seem to be there, don't let it convince you to quit. Learn from it and move on.

Case in point, I was invited by Guinness World Records to perform on a television show called *Guinness World Records Gone Wild.* Since there was no official "Guinness" world record concerning glass breaking, I was a shoe-in. All they asked is to see how fast it would take for me to break three wine glasses. No sweat, I knew I'd knock it out in four or five minutes. (Remember, I use Schott Zwiesel, not rinky dinky glasses, and even after shattering several hundred, they're still hard to break.) The only condition I required was to perform in a controlled environment, one without echo, such as a non-resonant studio, or if outside, somewhere without lots of reflective surfaces, as exterior resonant sources can affect the glass.

When I showed up on set, I saw a tent, which I assumed was for me. However, I was told I would be performing in an airplane bunker. I knew from the echo that it would affect my performance, but I figured I'd just have to up the decibels. Imagine my surprise when I am called on stage and told that in order to set the world record, I would have to shatter three glasses in less than sixty seconds.

Being a professional, I hid the nervousness from my face. Sixty seconds is barely time to warm up my glass-breaking scream, let alone shatter one glass. Still, I tried, screaming at one glass, slapping it down on the table, grabbing another, etc.

Needless to say, I didn't break one single glass. After 145 successful attempts before this particular show, I finally broke my winning streak. But, honestly, I wasn't upset. I was very disappointed in Guinness and the producers of the show for not following my guidelines, considering I am the champion of glass breaking, but it didn't unsettle me. I handled it well in the post-show interview and kept a smile on my face. My vocal coach, Elizabeth Sabine, was with me as well as Anne Loader McGee, my co-author for the *Sing Out Loud* series. Both were proud of me, regardless.

In the end, that one performance doesn't represent who I am, nor does it affect my future as a singing, glass-breaking vocal coach, because I choose not to be defined by one performance when I've traveled the globe shattering glasses in Europe, China, and Japan.

So, when you reflect on a gig where you're thrown off your game, don't let it define you. Push on and push hard. But in the end, always do your best. You are the front man and you must give your all. Speaking of being a front man, my student/friend Ben Carroll knows as well as anyone how scary it can first be to step out in front of the limelight, but Ben handles it like the pro he is. So I asked Ben to share his thoughts on being the best you can be on stage. Take it away, Ben.

IT'S ALL IN YOUR MIND
By Ben Carroll

It's all in your mind. So much of singing in a rock band is about attitude, it's really important that you don't psych yourself out.

I've been a professional musician for over a decade now, but I've only recently made the leap to singing lead vocals. The truth is, even for someone that has played thousands of shows to audiences of all sizes, taking center stage and being the mouthpiece for a band can still be a nerve-wracking experience. But it doesn't have to be. Being prepared and having a regular preshow routine can put you in the right frame of mind.

No thinking

First and foremost, your show should be well rehearsed. If you are to the point where you are on stage performing in front of an audience, then you do not want to be thinking about specific parts. I've always told my students that "thinking is a musician's enemy." What I mean by this is that you need to rehearse your music to the point where it can flow from you. You can't still be thinking (or worse, worrying) about the mechanics of what you are playing or singing come performance time. Readiness is absolutely key to nailing it live, because thinking on stage can lead to undermining your confidence, and a singer without confidence cannot put on a fully charged show. You've got to be ready to flow so you can give the full-on emotional delivery that your music deserves.

Warm up

I always warm up before a show. Warming up is not just about getting the blood flowing to your vocal cords and getting your voice to that sweet spot. It's also about getting yourself into the right head space to put on a great show. I keep a copy of Jaime's *Voice RX* in my car, in the band van, AND in my backpack so I never find myself without it preshow. (Actually, I have two copies in my car.) About 45 to 60 minutes before set-time, I head out to my car or the band van to warm up. This isn't just a chance to warm up my voice, it's also the time I use to collect my thoughts, home in on last bits of thinking that I may need to do before I get onstage (so I'm not thinking onstage!), focus on my breathing, and get myself into the head space that I need to be in so that I can put on a killer show.

I always do the same preshow warm-up so that it's not anything new. There is comfort in a familiar routine, and that will relax your mind and therein get rid of any preshow jitters you may have. Unfortunately, there is not always the time or the place to sneak away and warm up your voice in seclusion. When this happens I do Lip Bubbles to the opening band's music or to the house music on the PA while I focus on my breathing, and everything turns out great. =)

The Rescue Remedy

Jaime turned me on to Bach's Rescue Remedy. It's a flower extract that I use before every show to help reduce excess tension in my body. A few sprays of this can help to ease away your tension. Remember, tension in your body is really bad for your voice. Bach's Rescue Remedy is easy to find. I actually purchase it right at my local grocery store. It's very subtle, but it works wonderfully. I've found that it's best for me to use this more than an hour before showtime. If I take it too close to set-time, I find that my mind can wander while I'm onstage.

Bach's helps me with the most stressful part of performance, which for me is setting up the stage and getting ready to hit. It's always a mad rush to get your gear on stage and set up, and this is usually happening just minutes before you have to play your set. Not ideal for maintaining a good head-space, not ideal at all, ha-ha! But if you are stressing out about loading in and setting up your gear, then you may be in danger of carrying that into your show and having it affect your vocal performance. I've found Bach's can keep me from tensing up too much from the stress of load-in and setup.

It's your audience

Working an audience is something you learn how to do over time, and part of being a performer is finding your own way to work the audience. This is an art in and of itself. But the thing to remember is that an audience is there because they want to be entertained. They want you to be good. If you are afraid of the audience or if you get discouraged for any reason, you can lose an audience. It is always very important that you put on a show no matter how big your audience is. It doesn't matter if there are three people or a crowd of 30,000, make your performance count. Keep your confidence, keep your focus, and remember it's all in your mind. If you can rock an audience of three, then 30,000 will be a breeze.

@*#$% **Gasp** It's okay to make mistakes?

Mistakes happen. No matter how much you rehearse, no matter how confident and relaxed you are, mistakes can still happen. Just remember it's okay to make a mistake. The best thing to do is not even acknowledge the fact that you've made a mistake. Ninety-nine percent of the time the audience will never even notice, unless YOU point it out. Reacting to a mistake is the worst thing you can do. As a music teacher I always yell at my students for acknowledging their mistakes, not for making them. The most common thing to do is to make a bad face, and the worst thing to do is stop completely. No. No no no. Ha-ha! As you get to be a better and more confident musician, you'll realize that great musicians still make mistakes, but they are not only great musicians, they've gotten pretty good at making mistakes too. Learn to play/sing right through your mistakes and the audience will rarely notice when you do mess up.

It's all in your mind

Remember, it all comes down to attitude. If you are well rehearsed and prepared, warmed up and ready, and in a relaxed and confident state of mind, all you need to do to put on a great show is stay out of your own way. Let it flow.

Ben Carroll is a guitarist, vocalist, songwriter, instrumental artist, teacher, and a perpetual student of music. With a successful music career that spans the last decade, starting with Ra as a lead guitarist, two albums of instrumental guitar music, and now his newest project, The Hollow Glow, where he is singing lead vocals for the first time, Ben has had experience on all levels of the music industry. Ben is very busy recording and touring, Ra and The Hollow Glow are both still active, and he also still finds the time to teach on a regular basis and study voice with Jaime Vendera. Learn more about Ben and his music at bencarrollmusic.com.

To make sure that you are your best and *are* on your game, I want to turn over this chapter to my good friend Lonnie Winters for another great way to prepare you for the show. Take it away, Lonnie.

PRE-GIG MIND & BODY CLEANSE

By Lonnie Winters

Your band goes on stage in an hour. You've been fighting a sinus headache all afternoon. Now it's 30 minutes before showtime and you have a full-blown sinus headache. You know that every time you belt out a high note it will feel like your head is going to explode, like Jim Carey doing a Michael Bolton impression. Why did this happen? How could you have prevented this from happening? The "whys" are not the main concern at the moment; how to remedy the problem is the focus—and I've got the answer.

Find a quiet place; lie down; find a pillow, towel, or even a bunched up hoodie to prop up your head, and I'll show you a ten-minute self-massage lymphatic drainage session that will not only clear your sinus cavities but also reduce your preshow anxiety. This technique is so powerful for clearing the lymphatic system, as well as your mind, that it can also be used to knock out insomnia. By following the simple diagrams in this article, you will be able to reduce the chance of making your opening night a head-splitting nightmare.

Like harmonizing with a choir, timing is crucial. But first let me explain what is actually happening during your session. Unlike the cardiovascular system, the lymphatic system does not have its own propulsion system. Blood is pumped through blood vessels by the heart. (Thank you, Captain Obvious.) Interstitial (lymph) fluid is propelled through the lymph vessels by the reservoir (vibration) of the blood moving the veins and arteries. During this session, your fingertips will become the lymphatic system's heart. This is a very light but extremely powerful technique. If you have any ailments other than sinus obstruction, consult with a physician before administering this modality.

First let's address the pressure. As you're lying down, place a nickel on your forehead and memorize the weight of the coin. This is all the pressure you will use during the session. We are working with the lymphatic system, which lies just under the skin. For the duration of this session, forget anything you might have heard about trigger points, acupressure points, or reflexology. This is something completely different. The muscles are not factored into this routine. Pressure is the key factor. If too much pressure is used, it will not work.

Think of the lymphatic system like a swimming pool with several drains (watersheds). Whenever you see "watershed" listed in the sequences below, just know that you are clearing a path for the water (lymph vessels) to drain into the lymph nodes and out to the bloodstream. As far as the pathway of the lymphatic system, just remember that lymph vessels (the water entering the pool) drain to lymph nodes (the pool filter), which drain into the bloodstream (filtered pool water). This is a continuous cycle.

If you're ready to begin, you should now be lying on your back with a pillow under your head. Follow each sequence in order:

Sequence One: Supraclavicular Watershed
1. Cross your arms in a vampiric pose.
2. Place your fingertips just above your collar bones on each side, about an inch from the sternocleidomastoid distal attachments.
3. With a nickel's weight of pressure, move your fingertips inward (lateral to medial, not anterior to posterior.) Repeat this very slowly ten times.
4. Move your fingertips an inch from the first position and repeat. Move your fingertips an inch from the second position and repeat.

Sequence Two: Anterior Cervical Watershed

1. Place your fingertips on the sides of your neck right where the neck meets the shoulders (first position). Perform ten circles by first pushing up, back, down. Remember, this is a pumping action circle. Stop. Circle. Stop.
2. Move fingertips one inch above first position. Repeat ten times.
3. Move fingertips one inch above second position. Repeat ten times.

Sequence Three: Submandibular Watershed

1. First Position—Place your hands in a prayer pose. Now place the tips of your first three fingers (not the thumb) under your chin. Slowly, with a nickel's weight of pressure, open your hands like a book. Open. Rest. Close. Repeat ten times.
2. Second Position—Move your fingertips one inch away (medial to lateral) from the first position. Open. Rest. Close. Repeat ten times.
3. Third Position—Move your fingertips one inch away (medial to lateral) from the second position. Open. Rest. Close. Repeat ten times.

Sequence Four: Sideburns

1. First Position—Move your fingertips to your jawline on both sides (bilaterally). Imagine you are beginning on the bottom of your sideburns. Make ten circles by first pushing up, back, down. Remember, this is a pumping action. Circle. Stop. Circle. Stop.
2. Second Position—Move fingertips one inch above first position. Repeat ten times.
3. Third Position—Move fingertips one inch above second position. Your fingertips should end evenly in line with your earlobes. Repeat ten times.

*Optional—You may continue this sequence up to the temporal bones if desired.

Sequence Five: Chin

1. First Position—Place first and second fingertips on your chin, just below your lower lip (bilaterally). Make ten circles by first pushing up, back, down.
2. Second Position—Place first and second fingertips next to the corners of your mouth (bilaterally.) Make ten circles by first pushing up, back, down.

Sequence Six: Mustache

1. Position One—Place fingertips under your nose (three inches lateral from the middle of the upper lip.) With a nickel's weight of pressure, gently move fingertips in a medial to lateral direction ten times.
2. Position Two—Place fingertips one inch laterally away from first position and repeat.
3. Position Three—Place fingertips one inch laterally away from second position and repeat.

Sequence Seven: Nasal Sinuses

1. Revert back to the vampiric pose, only higher this time.
2. Position One—Place your first fingertips on both sides of your nose. Actually, your fingers will be on your face right beside the ala (the structure that houses your nostrils) of the nose. Move your fingers in circles (up-out-down or superior-lateral-inferior) ten times with a nickel's weight of pressure.
3. Position Two—Place fingertips on either side of the nose. (This is the dorsum of the nose.) Push fingertips inferior (downward) ten times.
4. Position Three—Place fingers one inch above position two. (Your fingertips should almost be in your eyes.) Push fingertips inferior ten times.

Sequence Eight: Cheekbones

1. First Position—Place fingertips on your cheekbones. Move fingertips in a circular motion (superior-lateral-inferior) ten times.
2. Second Position—Move fingertips one inch lateral and one inch inferior from first position. Move fingertips in a circular motion (superior-lateral-inferior) ten times.

Sequence Nine: Brows

1. First Position—Place thumb and first finger on the lateral edge of both eyebrows (Don't know what lateral means yet? Shame on you!!!) Your fingers should be in a pinching position, but do NOT pinch. You should only apply a nickel's weight of pressure, remember? Now, with the lateral edge of your brows gently engaged, pull them laterally ten times.

2. Second Position—Place thumb and first fingertip one inch medially away from first position and gently pull brows laterally ten times.
3. Third Position—Place thumb and first fingertip one inch medially away from second position and gently pull brows laterally ten times.

Sequence Ten: Headband

1. First Position—Lay the full length of your four fingers (of each hand) on both sides of your forehead. With a nickel's weight of pressure, move both hands laterally ten times.
2. Second Position—Move the full length of your four fingers (of each hand) on both sides of your forehead one inch laterally from first position. With a nickel's weight of pressure, move both hands laterally ten times.
3. Third Position—Move the full length of your four fingers (of each hand) on both sides of your forehead one inch laterally from second position. With a nickel's weight of pressure, move both hands laterally ten times.

Sequence Eleven: Temporal/Macaulay

1. Place both hands on both sides of your head. Think Macaulay Culkin in *Home Alone.* Now, just move your hands all the way up the sides of your head until your fingertips meet at the top of your head. (You big hair guys may not want to do this part if you have already been to hair and makeup.)
2. Now, simply compress your hair in an inferior (downward) direction ten times. *Repeat Sequences 7 and 9 as desired. These sequences are the

"hot spots" where most of the congestion occurs. It is a good idea to revisit these sequences for better results.

The results of your first lymphatic session may vary. Most describe a tickling sensation over the entirety of the areas worked, followed by a sensation of easier breathing with a breath of clean air. I have performed this modality hundreds of times on several individuals over the past seven years. The feedback has been 98 percent positive and 2 percent "I guess it worked. I don't know."

Some people just don't like to give feedback. I have had clients tell me that the results are immediate; they feel it working within seconds after I begin the session. Some have commented that they begin to breathe better on their way home from their appointment, which is very important for singers. But the results you experience depend on several factors. If you have a headache because you are dehydrated, haven't eaten enough, or have more serious issues, then you will probably not get a lot out of this session. So stay hydrated, don't starve yourself, and address any serious health concerns.

As a singer, you ARE your instrument, so take care of your instrument. Just remember to move slowly through the movements, breathe steadily, monitor your pressure, relax, and perform this session daily. It is extremely important for every singer to keep their sinuses clear and their lymphatic system moving smoothly. So, until my next publication, breathe clear and sing even more so.

Lonnie Winters, LMT, was a progressive metal bass player for 15 years before he decided to dedicate his hands to massage therapy. Lonnie has been a professional licensed massage therapist since 2005. Lonnie began training in Specialized Deep Tissue massage therapy immediately after graduating with honors from the Collins Career Center Massage Therapy Program in November of 2004. Since that time, he has studied PNF stretching, ortho-bionomy, myofascial release, and advanced trigger point techniques. In 2009 he completed a 12-month surgical technology certification program to better treat his post-surgical clients. As well, he is certified in advanced myoskeletal alignment techniques, all of which qualify him as a medical massage therapist. Having been employed by several medical clinics throughout Kentucky and Ohio, he has worked closely with doctors, nutritionists, physical therapists, occupational therapists, and surgeons. He is currently working on a series of training manuals and videos covering various massage techniques to benefit all musicians. He can be reached at LonnieWinters@gmail.com.

REVISITING THE STUDIO

Ah, back to the studio. I'm not going to lie, I HATE recording because I'm a perfectionist and I always feel I can do a better take or create a better melody. But, as an artist, recording is inevitable. Eventually, people are going to want to hear you. Nowadays, almost anyone can make a great home recording in their bedroom with the advent of software and affordable recording equipment. Though I'm not going to cover recording tips, because there are hundreds of books dedicated to the subject, I will offer up a few personal tips and tell you what I'm using for my studio setup to record audio files for my books, screaming programs, and songs.

Before we move on, I think it's important to note that if you plan to begin recording your own music, you MUST sing every day so that your songs feel like second nature by the time you start recording. I light-sing our catalog of originals every day while jogging in the morning. Singing at rehearsal is NOT enough, as my students already know, considering I request that they sing every day for a minimum of one-third longer than their typical gig. So, if your gig is forty-five minutes long, you need to sing an hour a day after your warm-up and workout. If you aren't regularly performing, you should still sing for the same amount of time as your workout. If your workout is thirty minutes long, be ready for thirty minutes of singing followed by a quick cool-down.

When you begin singing every single day, I suggest recording yourself. Your cell phone recorder will do fine. Hearing yourself will open your creative mind to a wide variety of possibilities, especially if you're singing your own songs. It also serves to help you to discover and correct flaws in your voice, such as flat notes or sloppy vocal runs.

Now on to my various recording setups. I must say that I enjoy recording vocals in my own home because I have so many ideas for the speaking parts of training programs and melodies for our songs that I eat up a lot of recording time in the studio.

I understand your home recording rig will be based on affordability, so let's discuss some options. I've used a variety of programs, microphones, and effect processors over the years. Some worked, some didn't. Currently, for my home setup, I use Reaper (reaper.fm) and Presonus Studio One for recording. I also own Sonar, which I've use for some our screaming programs, so that I can share sessions with my screaming product producer. When I'm playing around with new ideas, I actually prefer the customizability of Reaper. Reaper doesn't cause my computer to lag as Sonar has in the past, and Reaper is as easy to use as Pro Tools.

Cost wise, Reaper is free, though you can upgrade the program for under one hundred bucks, and it will work as well as the others. Sonar and Studio One can cost several hundred dollars, while Pro Tools LE can run from a few hundred up toward a thousand. There are other great programs as well. I suggest you review them all, and if you will be using a studio and working with the same producer, it would be best if you had the same multitrack recording software as your producer so that you can share files. Yes, you can still work together on different DAWs by exchanging the WAV files and lining them up at 0, but it's much easier when you can also share the session file so that all the tracks perfectly line up.

Now for the brain hub that will run your recording program—your computer. If at all possible, use a desktop as opposed to a laptop. Also, use an external hard drive to record and store your audio files. I have a laptop with a quad core and eight gigs of RAM, but the video card seems to add to the latency, causing me to have to mix the music files down to a mono track before I record the vocals. So I bought a desktop strictly for recording to resolve the issue.

I use the external hard drive because recording right to your main hard drive forces your computer to read, record, and store all at the same time all within the same system. An external hard drive solves this problem, and they're very affordable.

To get me into the computer, I use a simple Alesis io2 USB connector, and it seems to do fine for my purposes. I did at first have some issues with Reaper recognizing the Alesis io2, but installing ASIO4ALL (asio4all.com) solved the problem. This is just one of countless interfaces that can be used. You may prefer something a little simpler or even  higher end, possibly a dedicated fire wire box for this job for faster speeds. Choose what works for you.

As far as affordable microphones, I found the Rode NT1-A to be a good choice for recording in a home studio. I've also used an Audio Technica 4033 mic and a Blue Bluebird microphone. Both were clean, bright, with perfect clarity for the speaking voice.

I've used more expensive microphones in the studio, like the Blue Bottle. It has interchangeable capsules, which allows an engineer to play around with the sound to find just the right sound for a singer.

Bluebird   **Blue Bottle**   **Blue Bottle Capsules**

Since I tend to sing so loud, I've easily distorted both the NT1-A and Bluebird, but partially corrected this after my good friend James Lugo suggested I flip the microphone upside down and then set the capsule at nose level. (Learn more about this mic technique in the Q&A section of James's book, *Vocal Insanity.*) Still, with the decibels I was cranking out, it pushed the limits of both mics. Not wanting to spend thousands to own my own Blue Bottle, Sahaj Ticotin turned me onto a company called Studio Projects, makers of the C1 microphone. This three-hundred-dollar microphone works as well as a microphone ten times the price. It solved my problem of overpowering the mic when recording vocals at home. I ended up choosing the CS1 for the fact that it had more control over the audio parameters. For example, I can change the polar patterns and pad the mic if needed. They also offer the CS5 for more polar patterns.

C1   CS1   CS5

For compression and preamp, I decided to go for an affordable voice channel that does it all. Many engineers prefer single units. I've used single units, such as the old faithful Alesis 3630 for compression, which always worked great for me.

For preamps, I've used everything from the preamp on my TC Helicon VoiceLive 2 to the Avalon VT747SP. I used the latter in Nashville when working with Dallan Beck. The TC units are under a grand, while the Avalon may cost over twice as much. My favorite affordable preamp is the Studio Projects VTB1. It is a very unique

preamp that allows you to use solid state or tube or a blend of both. Like the SP microphones, the VTB1 is very affordable at less than two hundred dollars and worth five times as much.

If you want to record at home and prefer to invest the dollars you'd spend in the studio in an affordable voice channel, there are a wide variety of affordable units on the market. The ART Voice Channel is very affordable at under three hundred dollars.

As you know, I am a huge TC Helicon fan, so if you can swing a few more hundred, you should check out the VoiceLive rack.

I personally own the discontinued Joe Meek One Q channel strip. I was quite surprised by the One Q's tone. In my mind, I needed a tube preamp, but the Joe Meek is surprisingly warm and does some pretty cool things sonically with the compressor. Still, I have a VTB1 for that tube sound.

When I've recorded in a professional studio, I've used a Manley VoxBox. This is a top of the line pro unit costing around six grand, but is well worth the money because it can handle any vocal input no matter how loud or brutal and produces a very warm, clean tone. Which brings up a point. If you're going to record in a studio, find an engineer that works with you. Bottom line, if the Manley VoxBox doesn't fit your home recording budget, invest in one of the previously mentioned affordable models, and simply buy studio time to use higher end gear.

Before investing a dime, I suggest you listen to audio examples of different vocal preamps, compressors, and channel strips in your price range. Once you find units you like, do a simple Internet search to see if you can find each used or refurbished to save money. You may be able to upgrade to a more expensive unit when buying it used. However, always research the sellers rating before purchasing.

Now that you have a channel strip, you have to learn to work it. I also thought compression was the key. Not so. In fact, nowadays, you don't even need a compressor during the actual recording. But it still boils down to how you set the preamp. The key is to get a solid signal that doesn't distort on your loud notes (though a little distortion is cool in tube preamps), and then use the compressor to tame the very loudest notes if an only if you need it. If using compression, you better understand the beast. Compression eludes many, so as a starting point I suggest both a fast attack and release, starting at around a ratio of 3:1. You can record a few takes and see how it's working with your voice. For the output, you'll have to do a live run and pop the compressor in and out of the chain to adjust the output, because you want the compressed output to sound the same in levels as without compression. Again, compression is to smooth it all out, unless you want to pump the sound for a breathy tone, in which case you could bump up the ratio to say 7:1 or higher. Dallan Beck covers the basics of setting compression in *Raise Your Voice*. Follow his advice and you'll master compression in no time.

As well, you might want to use EQ to fill out the voice (though it is probably wisest to run flat and add EQ post production). Again, I'm not an engineer and you'll learn more from studio recording manuals and experimentation. But a few EQ pointers to get you started are:

- Use a high-pass filter to cut the frequencies below 80hz to get rid of unwanted low noise such as fans and passing cars. This will also help tame the Ts and Ps that pop the sound.
- To eliminate a bit of nasality, cut a few db around 1khz.
- To add some clarity, slightly boost the frequencies around 4khz–6khz.
- To remove harshness, you can slightly cut the frequencies between 2khz–4khz.

These are just generic examples. Remember, EQ is an ear thing, so it's your choice. It truly takes some practice to zone in on the correct setting for your voice. There are so many factors that affect these settings, including the microphone you're using and the channel strip's capabilities. And the most elusive has always seemed to be the compressor. So to help you out further, I've invited our good friend Dallan Beck back to help you "tune in" your compression settings. Go for it, Dallan.

UNDERSTANDING BASIC VOCAL COMPRESSION
By Dallan Beck

Listen closely. Take critical notes. Make important adjustments. Repeat. It's very simple, except for the fact that no one told me *what* to listen for. That's the all-important key. What are you listening for? If you're just looking for knob settings and presets, you are not listening. I'm not saying that presets aren't great sometimes.

For me, every recording is different. The mystery and drive is all about solving the puzzle, and knowing *why* the sound becomes what I want it to be.

So let's start by just recording a "dry" vocal. This is using your microphone, plugging it into a microphone preamp, and setting levels. Just make sure that your mic preamp setting isn't too high. You'll know it's too high if at any point in the vocal performance, your recorded track "clips" or "goes into the red." I'm going to assume that you are all recording digitally, and that means not reaching 0 dbfs (decibels full scale) on your audio track's meter.

This may take a couple of tries. Be patient. Take your time. If your levels are too low or too high, it becomes the first problem in a domino effect of problems. It's okay if your highest levels are 3–6db below their peaking point. I don't want you to try to find the last tenth of a decibel of headroom before clipping begins. At the same time, don't record so low that you never even see the meter move above the -10db point. What's going to happen if you record too low is that you're not able to really hear all of the recorded information in the track. This will be a problem later when it comes to mixing.

Once you've recorded your vocal with "good" levels, the listening process is crucial. Now there are two sets of ears. The Producer's ears and the Engineer's ears. The Producer's ears should hear all of the musical questions and answers:

> Was this a great performance?
> Was there an emotional connection to the lyric?
> How was the phrasing?
> How were the melodies?
> How was the vocal technique?
> Etc., etc.

There could be an entire book written on just the Producer's role with a vocal recording. That's not the intention of this article. We are going to focus on the Engineer's ears. However, I need to stress that the Producer's role is critical in allowing the Engineer to succeed at his/her role. Have you ever heard the phrase "polishing a turd"? That's where it comes from. Engineers are technicians. We can only mold the clay we are given. It is up to the Producer to make sure that the "clay" is not just a lump of formless dirt.

So I am going to make a huge leap of faith that the Artist and the Producer have done their jobs well. I realize that it's probably not the case, but I have to start somewhere. So when does compression come in?

If you're listening to your recording and you notice that the volume of the vocal is changing too much in relationship to the track, you might be in need of a compressor. Of course, vocal technique goes a long way to controlling unnecessary volume changes, but that's also not the discussion for this article.

Backing away from the mic and moving closer to the mic will adjust the volume swings, but they also create other problems, like room reflections and proximity effect.

So, with that out of the way, I just want to make sure that you are "hearing" the volume changes and "deciding" that they are not improving the quality of the song in a positive way. Controlling the "dynamics" (volume changes) can make your vocal sound more professional, stronger, bigger, and tighter. Words and inflections will not be lost in the mix of the track. The idea is to focus the vocal volume to be "ever present" without losing a sense of feeling.

The way that I learned how to use a compressor was actually not by using one at all. I used to have to "ride" the faders on the console. That's just a fancy way of saying that I had to try to raise/lower the volume for everything that I thought needed to be louder or softer.

I always force my students to really try this first before using a compressor. They will understand two things. One, what to listen for when using a compressor later. Two, how really difficult it is to make hundreds of changes on a fader! I'm not that accurate and I can hear faster than I can move something. Now, enter the compressor.

There are many different kinds of compressors and names for settings on compressors, so I am going to have to go with the most common. Most average compressors will consist of five basic features: ratio, threshold, attack, release, and gain/output.

The threshold control is honestly the most critical. This is deciding the volume level setting for the compressor to react to the signal. When your vocal gets louder than the threshold, the compressor reacts to try to keep the level from getting any higher. When your sound is below the threshold, the compressor should react and pass the original signal through without changing it.

Finding the threshold is an "ear thing" as well as an "eyeball" thing. You need to watch whatever meters/levels you have on your compressor and decide what volume level you believe to be "too loud." This is why it is important to record with strong, clear levels to start with.

But the threshold doesn't have the power to "pull down" the volume of the vocal. It's just the trigger point. It's what sets it on/off, so to speak. So what does control the amount of power the compressor can use to "pull down" the volume? It's the ratio. It's literally a comparison between how much level goes in versus how much comes out. A ratio of 1:1 does nothing to change the volume. But a ratio of 2:1 means that for every two decibels (volume measurements) the vocal goes above the threshold, only one decibel of volume change will be allowed. That in effect reduces the volume change above the threshold by 50 percent. A ratio of 4:1 creates a 75 percent reduction. A Ratio of 10:1 creates a 90 percent reduction, etc.

Basically, the higher the ratio, the more the compressor can "pull down" the level of the vocal as it goes over the threshold. For dramatic effect, using higher ratios (8:1 and up) creates these noticeable "ceilings" that vocal "smashes into" and isn't allowed to go much higher. Lower ratios are more "transparent" and less noticeable, because the change in level won't be as drastic. So, if you don't need a whole lot of volume change, then lower ratios are the first choice. If you need a lot of volume change from the original dynamic levels, then higher ratios are the first choice.

The problem is that when the sound is crossing the threshold all the time, the compressor is reacting, and that can cause "artifacts." You don't want people listening to your compressor, you want them listening to your vocal!

So attack and release are like fade times going into and out of compression. They are there to "smooth" the changing between the compressor turning on and turning off. The attack value is how many milliseconds it takes for the ratio to start working. It needs to be fast enough to not "miss" the vocal level change, but not so fast as to cause "pumping." That is the description of hearing the compressor's ratio starting to work. It's like you hear the sound "sucking backwards." It should smoothly change into compression without being obvious.

The same rule applies, but in reverse, for release. This is how long it takes the ratio to stop working. If the release is too quick you hear a "breathing" effect when the volume change returns to the original vocal level. If the release is too long, the compressor is still "pulling down" the vocal level, even though it's no longer too loud.

The last variable is where the MAGIC comes in. And that is the gain/level adjustment. Up to this point we have simply LOST volume. It's been pulled down, and that's not what I wanted at all. What I want to do is increase the output of the compressor in order to "make up" for any volume losses I've created. So there should be a gain reduction readout or meter. It will show you how much you've taken away. Basically you are going to "add it" back in. So while the compressor is pulling down the vocal 5db, it won't actually be getting quieter, the gain makeup will "counter" that action. So in the end, the loudest vocal sound will be returned to its original level.

Now that sounds confusing! Why go through all this work to pull down the volume, if all you are going to do is bring it back up anyway? The answer is that the real MAGIC in the compressor is that we are going to be bringing up the softer levels to get closer to the louder levels! That is how we make the vocal sound more consistent. We are closing the gap between loud and soft by holding the loud to a set standard and bringing the softer levels up closer to meet the louder levels.

This is why GOOD compression makes a vocal sound bigger. The normally too quiet levels start to have mass and volume again, like you sang them louder, but without having to push to get it. Nuances are now audible without having to exaggerate them in an unnatural way.

Okay, so you start out with the ratio at 1:1 (basically not allowing compression). The attack and release would each be set at an average time, not fast and not slow. You watch your vocal levels to decide where that threshold should be set, based on what is "too dynamic." At what point does the level change "too much"? Next, you'll need to adjust your ratio to start "pulling down" the level. If all you need is a 2:1 ratio, that's fine. If you need a higher ratio to get a stronger effect, then adjust it up. Make sure that the sound is not getting "squashed." If it is, then maybe your attack and release need to adjusted, or your ratio is too high. When you finally dial it in, look at your gain reduction (GR) meter to see how hard the compressor worked. You'll need to adjust the gain/output level in order to get back what you lost. If at all possible, try to A/B the comparison between before and after the usage of compression. If you did it right, your vocal will be bigger and better!

It's a lot to take in, but be patient and above all, listen. The key has always been listening. The puzzle will always be what to *listen for.*

Dallan Beck is the former head instructor at SAE Nashville and the former director of the Recording Institute at MI in Los Angeles. He is the author of the Musicians Guide to Recording Series *for Hal Leonard Publications.*

Okay, back to my setup, ha-ha. Finally, I use the Vocal Booth Pro from Editors Keys to keep ambient noise from flowing into my vocal recordings. I actually recorded some of these audio files close to our air conditioner in our basement, as well as next to the computer, yet you don't hear either.

If you're going to do some home recording, research all the brands of equipment you'll need, read reviews, head to a music store to test some equipment, or rent pieces of equipment to test in your own studio before making a decision. If you're on a tight budget, but you really want to start honing your recording chops and playing with processors, there are many software programs to get you started. Even easier, if you're an iPad/iPhone user, there are some amazing apps for recording and adding vocal effects by TC Helicon, IK Multimedia, and 4 Pockets Audio.

Check out the VocaLive app by IK Multimedia. This app is a vocal effects processor with in-app purchases to expand your setup.

VocaLive   **Voice Jam Studio**

TC Helicon also offers great apps the VoiceJam Studio app that features software versions of their vocal effects line.

If recording is your thing, check out Meteor Multitrack Recorder, which is a full-fledged multitrack recorder for the iPad. I've recorded songs on my iPad for Vendera Vocal Academy using Meteor and other apps such as DRUMS XD for our midi programmed drums, Amplitube by IK Multimedia for my guitarist to bypass his amp, and iGrand Piano. All of these apps will help you to improve your singing, effect tweaking, and recording skills, and they're much more affordable a choice if you're just starting out.

If you're recording on an iPad, you may need an iRig Pro mic preamp which plugs into your lightning insert so you can use a condenser microphone. For more inserts, you may want a recording interface such as the Alesis iO DOCK. Either interface works with any recording app available to record directly to your iPad.

I personally use the iRig Pro by IK Multimedia to get my microphone signal into Meteor. The iRig Pro is basically a preamp that plugs into the lightning cable power insert that delivers a solid, clean signal from my CS1/VTB1 into the iPad.

That wraps it up for Stage & Studio and pretty much the whole book. In other words, that's all folks. But before I leave you high and dry, I'd like to discuss a few ways to approach these new exercises to give you the best possible scenario for keeping your voice in shape. So, to finish the book, I've added new vocal routines to give you a day-by-day, play-by-play guide to take you from Karaoke singer to superstar. Let's blast off to the last chapter.

REVISITING YOUR DAILY VOCAL ROUTINE

NOW IT'S TIME TO LINE YOU out for your future vocal workouts. I'll cover a new exercise routine in several workouts, to cover an easy, medium, and hardcore workout as well as a maintenance program for the singer who just needs to keep their voice in shape on the road. I call these routines the Karaoke Singer, Gigging Musician, Aspiring Rockstar, Touring Artist, and Isolation Freak. First things first: You must go through the following five-week training program before switching to one of the four workouts.

FIVE-WEEK KICK STARTER PROGRAM

To master the Ultimate Isolation Exercise, you must spend weeks in practice before it feels normal. Thus, I've designed a five-week program covering twenty-eight days (the amount of time it takes to make or break a habit). Considering we're developing muscle, I've factored in some rest days for the 28-day regimen. ALWAYS start your morning with my suggested shower workout, to wake your voice up with some VSR and one of my warm-up mp3s while steaming. I think the morning warm-up is one of the best things a singer can do for their voice to prepare them for the day ahead. Follow the Kick Starter program and you'll have mastered the Ultimate Isolation Exercise in five weeks, and then you'll be ready to change to one of the workout programs that best suits your needs. Here is a breakdown of the following five weeks:

Week 1
Perform the Ultimate Isolation Exercise beginning dynamically soft as follows:
* Monday—Yah (Think "Ah" on Lip Bubbles, Resonant Hums, and Gargling Tone.)

* Tuesday—Yay (Think "A" on Lip Bubbles, Resonant Hums, and Gargling Tone.)
* Wednesday—Yee (Think "E" on Lip Bubbles, Resonant Hums, and Gargling Tone.)
* Thursday—Yoh (Think "Oh" on Lip Bubbles, Resonant Hums, and Gargling Tone.)
* Friday—You (Think "Oo" on Lip Bubbles, Resonant Hums, and Gargling Tone.)
* Saturday—Perform all five vowels for every pitch before moving to the next pitch.
* Sunday—Rest.

Week 2

Perform the Ultimate Isolation Exercise beginning dynamically loud as follows:
* Monday—Yah (Think "Ah" on Lip Bubbles, Resonant Hums, and Gargling Tone.)
* Tuesday—Yay (Think "A" on Lip Bubbles, Resonant Hums, and Gargling Tone.)
* Wednesday—Yee (Think "E" on Lip Bubbles, Resonant Hums, and Gargling Tone.)
* Thursday—Yoh (Think "Oh" on Lip Bubbles, Resonant Hums, and Gargling Tone.)
* Friday—You (Think "Oo" on Lip Bubbles, Resonant Hums, and Gargling Tone.)
* Saturday—Perform all five vowels for every pitch before moving to the next pitch.
* Sunday—Rest.

Week 3

Perform the Ultimate Isolation Exercise as follows:
* Monday—Perform all five vowels dynamically soft for every pitch before moving to the next pitch.
* Tuesday—Perform all five vowels dynamically loud for every pitch before moving to the next pitch.
* Wednesday—Perform all five vowels dynamically soft for every pitch before moving to the next pitch.
* Thursday—Perform all five vowels dynamically loud for every pitch before moving to the next pitch.

* Friday—Perform all five vowels dynamically soft for every pitch before moving to the next pitch.)
* Saturday—Perform all five vowels dynamically loud for every pitch before moving to the next pitch.
* Sunday—Rest.

Week 4

Perform the Ultimate Isolation Exercise on all five vowels for every pitch before moving to the next pitch as follows:
* Monday—Start dynamically soft.
* Tuesday—Start dynamically loud.
* Wednesday—Start dynamically soft.
* Thursday—Start dynamically loud.
* Friday—Perform the entire routine twice, dynamically soft the first round, dynamically loud the second round.
* Saturday and Sunday are rest days this week.

Week 5

* Monday–Friday—Perform the Ultimate Isolation Exercise dynamically soft on all five vowels for every pitch before moving to the next pitch. Stair-step the basic E-Scream exercise. Do not use the new E-Scream slide during the fifth week of the Kick Starter program. You must first get used to stair stepping before alternating your E-Screams. Finish by performing the Ultimate Isolation Exercise dynamically loud on all five vowels for every pitch before moving to the next pitch.
* Saturday and Sunday are rest days this week.

Note: Unless you perform your Isolation workout right after or within a few hours of your shower warm-up, you should perform Vocal Stress Release once again, adding Vocal Stage Prep if needed. Always cool down with the Voice & Body Cool Down. Once you've completed the five-week program, choose one of the following programs to fit your schedule:

KARAOKE SINGER

When you're just singing for fun and not in a serious band, I understand you may not be so worried about gaining massive range and power. So I suggest a basic warm-up consisting of Vocal Stress Release with the vocal warm-up program of your choice (*Voice RX, etc.)* to get you prepared for your weekend Karaoke gig. Perform the Ultimate Isolation Exercise five times a week as follows:

Monday—Yah as in "Father"
Tuesday—Yay as in "Play"
Wednesday—Yee as in "Sweet"
Thursday—Yoh as in "Toe"
Friday—You as in "Food"

Alternate the Ultimate Isolation Exercise every week, starting dynamically soft one week and dynamically loud the next week.

GIGGING MUSICIAN

A gigging musician requires more. The *Ultimate Vocal Warm Up* or a similar mp3 in my stable will work for warming up, but I also suggest adding the Mini-Siren or the advanced vocal cord stretch at the tail end of your warm-up an hour before your gig and rehearsals. For voice strengthening, practice the Ultimate Isolation Exercise Monday through Friday, a different vowel every day, alternating every other week between dynamically soft and dynamically loud.

If you're working on the super-high piercing notes, you may consider stair stepping the basic E-Scream exercise daily. If you're a lead screamer, add the Grit Siren or slip in some exercises from screaminglessons.com to hone your grit.

ASPIRING ROCKSTAR

Wanna be a rock star? Who doesn't? (Thanks again, Jim.) It's going to take LOTS of work. Here's the best way to ramp up your career.

Warm up in the morning with Vocal Stress Release and Vocal Stage Prep (in the shower if possible) as you sing along to one of my warm-up mp3s. After your morning warm-up, you must set aside two hours minimum from your day for practice. You'll perform the Ultimate Isolation Exercise six days per week. On each individual pitch, perform all five vowels before moving to the next pitch, starting soft one week, then loud the next week. This eliminates performing one vowel per day, because you'll cover the vowels on each pitch, each time you do the exercise. This is where the "One Exercise, One Minute, One New Voice" motto kicks in, because this will take roughly one minute per pitch to perform.

You're also going to add scales. *Jim Gillette's Vocal Power* scales (available at buildabettervoice.com) are the best. Once you've mastered Jim's scales, check out the advanced scales I've created, available through venderapublishing.com.

End with the advanced E-Scream slides and Grit Sirens if you need a grit workout. Whatever specialized exercises you feel you need for your type of singing, make sure to add them to your routine.

You need plenty of physical exercise too. Refer to all the exercise sections in *RYV 1 & 2*. Make sure to add some form of cardio such as skip bounding or the treadmill speed alternating. I also suggest adding my Total Body Cardio routine.

If you're already gigging, figure out the length of your set, then sing your set, adding a third extra songs to meet your daily singing requirements. If your set is forty-five minutes, you need to be singing an hour a day. You can sing your songs by light singing, as James Labrie does. Light singing trains the mind/body coordination for each pitch and vowel and will make singing at full blast much easier. It may sound crappy when you first attempt light singing (singing so soft that it sounds like a fly is singing), but it will sound cleaner and clearer after a week or so of practice.

End with the Voice & Body Cool Down. Also, make sure to start a solid vocal health regimen to maintain your voice, including meeting your water quota.

TOURING ARTIST

I understand time is limited for the touring artist. Still, singing is demanding and so are all those interviews you must do. So I've created a seven-day routine to help keep the "on the road" singers in top vocal shape. Still, it's an easier program than the Aspiring Rockstar program.

Every day, start your morning with Vocal Stress Release and one of my warm-up mp3s, preferably in the shower, though I understand that's not always an option. But if you can hit the shower later in the day, repeat the process, because a hot shower will open up the lungs and voice and relax the muscles as you stretch.

Before hitting the stage, repeat Vocal Stress Release, adding Vocal Stage Prep, then warm up with the warm-up routine of your choice, regardless of whether it's tons of Lip Bubbles and Mini-Sirens, *Voice RX*, the *Ultimate Vocal Warm Up*, or one of the *Extreme Scream* warm-ups. The key is to know your voice, and only you know when you're warmed up. So take it one note at a time for as long as needed until you feel sufficiently warmed up.

On your days off (your nonshow days), add the Ultimate Isolation Exercise, singing every vowel per pitch. On the road, I'd start dynamically soft because it's more "warming up" as opposed to "working out" the voice, and we're more concerned with on-the-road vocal maintenance when touring. Slip in some *Vocal Power* scales if possible, and sing your set while light singing (easily done when traveling in your bunk in the back of the bus). If you are tired from the rigors of the road and feel you just need a vocal break, by all means, take that vocal break. Don't beat yourself up over a day of no singing or no practice. Relax and enjoy it, and take in some scenery to calm your mind and body. If you do want a little vocalizing on those days, simply slip in a few Lip Bubbles and elephants throughout the day.

I also suggest adding the Total Body Cardio routine, aka the Maximizer, some treadmill and/or skip bounding while touring, if possible. Hit the gym when you're at a hotel or hit the floor in your hotel room or on the tour bus for a few rounds of Total Body Cardio. FYI: Any of these exercises can be added to the other routines as well, because all singers need some sort of physical exercise to maintain overall body and vocal stamina.

ISOLATION FREAK

For those who want to focus purely on my Isolation exercises, I suggest you follow a program, six days a week as follows:

* Warm up in the shower in the morning with VSR and VSP while singing along to one of my mp3s.
* When it's time for your workout, start by performing the Ultimate Isolation Exercise dynamically soft, up and down the scale on all five vowels per pitch. Go immediately back to the Ultimate Isolation Exercise, starting dynamically loud, performing all five vowels per pitch working upscale, and then back down. ONLY work as high as comfortable and never forget to check for tension and pure tone with the "NO" and "YES" movements.
* Finish with E-Scream stair stepping. You can now perform E-Scream slides while stair stepping if preferred.
* Note how long it took to perform your entire workout, and then sing a variety of songs for at least the same length of time it took to perform your workout.
* Finish with the VBCD.
* Don't forget to slip in the Maximizer.

"So, which program do you follow, Jaime?" None, ha-ha. Remember, I created this system to make it easy for me to work out and warm up in minimal time. So I prefer to do the Ultimate Isolation Exercise on a vowel per day Monday through Friday, slipping in various programs such as *SingFit*, *Vocal Power* scales, even *Extreme Scream* programs, and individual Isolation exercises when working with newer students. I ALWAYS use one of my warm-up mp3s as my shower warm-up and before gigs. Bottom line, as a singer, we must be professional and always practice!

Professional singers need to practice and sing every day. Why exercise and sing every day? What if a professional body builder decided to slack off on their workouts at the gym? Their muscular definition would begin to deteriorate. If you want to keep your singing voice at peak level, you must exercise!

You may know some singers who don't warm up or work out and do fine. Good for them; they are the lucky few. But some of those "lucky few" who've been singing for twenty years will eventually begin to show signs of wear and tear. Hmmm, I wonder how they'd sound if they had exercised and cared for their voice all those years? They may have had another twenty years left in them! Wanna sing like you were twenty for the rest of your life? Keep your voice in shape with lots of practice. Speaking of which, here's my *Sing Out Loud* writing partner, Anne Loader McGee, to stress my point.

THE ART OF PRACTICE
By Anne Loader McGee

Co-authoring *Sing Out Loud Books I-IV* with Jaime Vendera and having studied for years with the famous Hollywood vocal coach Elizabeth Sabine, I've learned early the importance of practice. If the muscles needed for singing are not exercised daily, Elizabeth would say, the voice would not develop to its full potential. Consequently, this vocal coach's mantra of *Practice! Practice! Practice!* made perfect sense.

Let's face it; singers are lazy when it comes to a practice routine. What they don't realize is that skipping two or three days of practice can put you a week behind in progress, which is something you don't want. So here's a suggestion.

Grab a free app for your cell phone (an app like TUNED XD), then time your actual vocal routine. When you've finished with Jaime's Ultimate Isolation Exercise, continue on the E-Screams (or any other exercise you are doing) without stopping. When you've done ALL your vocal exercises, hit the stopwatch. How long did it take? Twenty minutes? Thirty? Forty-five? Whatever amount of time, that's the schedule you need to maintain with your current vocal routine. But make sure that with every timed workout you don't drift mentally and end up wasting minutes.

Another good trick is to find a "singing buddy." You agree to check with each other at a designated time each day to verify you have indeed practiced. Being accountable to someone else can be very motivating. You can call or email each other each day to see how long you've practiced, what notes you've reached, etc., to keep pushing yourselves to the top. By disciplining yourself with a timer you'll find yourself becoming faithful to your practice sessions. Place this reminder on a bunch of Post-It notes and stick them up in places where you'll see them constantly.

Anne Loader McGee is an award-winning children's writer. She has produced plays for young people, developed animation scripts, and had a number of short stories published in the Los Angeles Times and online magazines. She also authored The

Mystery at Marlatt Manor and Anni's Attic (children's fictional novels). Anne has studied voice with many well-known Hollywood vocal coaches. She co-wrote Strengthening Your Singing Voice with Elizabeth Sabine, a voice-strengthening expert whom many famous singers, actors, and speakers have consulted over the years. (elizabethsabine.net), and co-authored the young people's Sing Out Loud vocal training books I through IV with Jaime Vendera. You can find Anne McGee at annemcgee.com.

Follow Anne's advice and you'll skyrocket your vocal potential. And there you have it. Slip this manual into your gig bag alongside *RYV* and *SVH* and you'll be ready to rock! Alas, we've come to the end of the book. But before we end, I'd like to offer a great piece of advice and recap the main points of my system. First, I'd like to say that as you are developing your voice, you MUST rid your thoughts of the "I want it now" syndrome. The biggest complaint I hear from singers is, "I want it now … I want those high notes now … I want to be an amazing singer now." Vocal development takes time, plain and simple!

If I were a personal trainer and you came to me to develop six-pack abs, and I took you through an abdominal strength-training program, do you really think you'd exit the gym with six-pack abs that very day? Obviously, you said "No." So why in the world would you think you'd gain and master an extra octave in range after one training session? Believe it or not, that's a strong belief among beginning singers. And when a singer hasn't reached those high notes after a week or so of practice, many fall by the wayside and start slacking off on their workout routine. Then, a few months later, they complain about not having the voice they desire.

Vocal muscle is just like any other muscle. It will take lots of time and effort to build the muscle, so be patient. The key is to strive for your goals and work hard every day to reach those goals. Don't become disappointed when you don't have the tenor C or soprano A after a few sessions. Know that with every practice session you are gaining muscle. Think of it like a big, blank poster board that you add a star sticker to every time you practice. After you've placed 100 stars on your poster board from a legitimate practice session, I guarantee your voice will have grown closer to your goal.

So strive to practice and sing every day while keeping that end goal in mind, knowing it will be worth the wait to develop your voice. Now I'd like to recap just a few key points that you should observe while practicing and singing. This list is far from complete. You can add notes to this list that help you better practice and sing based on the writings in my books:

VENDERA'S KEY POINTS RECAP (WHEN SPEAKING & SINGING)

*Key Points for Vocal Technique
1. Breathe—Inhale down and out, expanding the belly, back, and ribs. Pretend that your floating ribs are fish gills opening out to your sides as you inhale.
2. Support—Push straight down to tighten the abdominals for supporting the tone. Do NOT grunt!
3. Placement—Always feel a buzzing sensation in the roof of the mouth. Remember, the sensation may feel as if it moves around from the front to the back depending on the vowel and the tone.

*Key Points when Vocalizing
1. When singing, take a micro-breath on a yawn to create the dome.
2. Allow the dome to change shape to the teepee on the higher notes.
3. Use the "YES" and "NO" movements to check for and to release vocal stress, as well as hone your tone.
4. Drink water all day to keep the vocal cords moist. Hot water in a thermos will help to reduce swelling. I drink hot water all day. I learned this from Tony Harnell and James Labrie, though Labrie does more warm water now.
5. ALWAYS sing and practice with passion and conviction, and ALWAYS have fun!!! Singing should be a passion, not a chore.

Follow these key points as you practice and sing and you'll build a rock-solid instrument. As a final note, I'd like to say that I believe in muscle confusion principles, which is one of the reasons I change up my warm-up routines, add *Vocal Power* scales, and at times refer back to my original Isolation exercises. This keeps the workout from becoming boring and allows you to exhaust the vocal muscles in different ways. For those who have asked, my program CAN be combined with other vocal routines. Any programs released through Vendera Publishing, such as programs by Elizabeth Sabine, James Lugo, Dr. Timothy Jameson, Valerie Bastien, and others, are perfectly acceptable and one hundred percent endorsed by me. I will not release a book or program that I do not back. So have a blast practicing and singing, feel free to experiment with programs I endorse, and email me when you release that amazing song!!!

Before ending *RYV2*, I'd like to say that the methods in my *RYV* series have worked for thousands of singers, and many times I have been asked "why" it works. My answer is simple-because it just does, ha-ha. However, for those yearning for a more serious answer to this question, I'd like to share one more article written by my close, personal friend, and fellow vocal coach, John Henny. John explains exactly why *RYV* has worked so amazingly well for thousands of singers. Take it away, John.

WHY IT WORKS: THE SCIENCE OF RYV
By John Henny

If you are reading this, then you are obviously a fan of Jaime Vendera and *Raise Your Voice*. If you've been doing the work in these two volumes then you are undoubtedly singing better as well. For most of us, that would be enough. But then they are the geeky few of us that like to lift the lid off of things, who take apart their radios and remote control cars, to see how and why things work. This chapter is for you.

A bit of a disclaimer, I'm a lowly voice teacher and in no way a researcher or scientist. I developed an interest in vocal science, especially acoustics and resonance, as I saw the remarkable power of vowel substitution and vowel control to make changes in my student's voices. The right vowel had an almost magical effect, immediately relieving strain, expanding range, and building power. How could very small adjustments make such a stunning difference?

I was led to discover what was happening and why it made such a huge effect on the voice. I read books and studied with some amazing minds, but I found I struggled with these concepts. It took many repeated readings and listenings to get this into my much smaller brain. I then spent quite a bit of time trying to find ways to make these concepts more understandable to other voice teachers and singers. I wish to share some of this with you here.

As a Vendera fan, you have come to enjoy his straightforward, no-frills approach to the very complex arena of singing. I will do my best to continue his BS-free style, and perhaps I'll break a wine glass when I'm done.

Sound

Sound waves, little vibrating molecules of air, that's what you have to musically offer as a singer. These sound waves - their complexity, intensity, speed, and perceived quality can either make you a James LaBrie — or the person being laughed out of an audition.

How are these molecules turned from standing air to making people stand and cheer for you? It's a three step process — air, vocal cords, and resonance. Resonance is the one we want to look at more deeply as its effect on the voice is only now being properly understood.

The Wave

Basically, air molecules are magnetically charged, which means they prefer to stay a certain distance from each other — kind of like their own personal space. When this personal space is violated, by forcing the molecules closer together, they react by pushing away from each other.

This starts a chain reaction of molecules bumping into each other, or vibrating. These vibrations come in waves ("sound wave", get it?). The number of waves we get per second gives us pitch. We measure these waves in Hertz, or HZ.

The standard tuning pitch is A440, which is the A above middle C on the piano. The 440 is the number of vibrations per second in this sound wave, also known as 440 Hz. In order to produce this A440, your vocal cords will open and close 440 times per second, creating 440 little pulses or waves of vibrating air. It is amazing to think that on this particular pitch, these waves occur 440 times per second.

On all pitches, your vocal cords will come together and close, in order to block the flow of air being pushed out of your lungs. This will create the building of pounds per square inch of air pressure as the molecules are squished together. The pressure will then overpower the cords, at which point they will open and let the compressed air out into the throat and mouth (your resonators).

The cords will again close to start the process over again. Hummingbirds beat their wings about 50 times per second, yet our vocal cords can do this open and closing process over 1000 times. Now that's fast!

Harmonics

This is the really cool part. The sound wave generated by your vocal cords is what we call a complex sound wave. This means it has lots of information in it, essentially a lot of pitches happening at the same time. We call each of these separate bits of information "harmonics.

Let's take the A below middle C on the piano. This is A220, since it is vibrating at 220 Hz. You will notice it is exactly half as fast as the A440, which is an octave above. This vibration at 220 Hz is actually just a small part of the sound wave. There are harmonics above 220. They occur at 440 Hz, 660 Hz, 880 Hz, etc. We hear the lowest harmonic at 220 Hz as the pitch and the harmonics above it as color. The upper harmonics are vibrating more quickly than the first harmonic and add brightness and bite to the sound.

Surely you have noticed the difference between a classical soprano and a female belting out Broadway songs. The classical singer dials back the upper harmonics to create the hollow, flute like sound while the Broadway belter dials them up, creating the bright, pingy belt. Dial them up and dial them down? How does one do this? The answer is: formants.

Formants

ForWHAT??? That's what I said when I first heard the word. I knew a bit about harmonics, but this formant stuff was a new concept entirely. What are formants? Well they're not really a thing – at least not one you can see (unless you are using spectrum analysis). They are rather a measurement of acoustical properties of a space. I know, it's still confusing.

Let's look at it this way. Have you ever been listening to loud music or a television in a room where certain notes cause things in the room to shake? For instance, a certain bass note causes the knickknacks on a shelf to vibrate.

This happens because the room you are in is boosting certain frequencies over others. Live sound engineers have to deal with this all the time. Concert venues will make certain frequencies louder than others, so the engineer has to dial these frequencies back on the soundboard, in order to create a balanced sound.

Let's say a room is boosting frequencies around 50 Hz. This means the size and shape of the room have come together to create a formant at 50 Hz. If the room is also boosting sound at 440 Hz, then there's a formant there as well. There can be, and often are, many formants in a room. Few rooms are without sound disturbing formants, and the ones that are usually found in very expensive recording studios.

Formants are the name given to these acoustic boosts. The formant will have a value which represents the part of the sound wave it is boosting, such as 200 Hz. They will also be numbered, the lowest value formant is the first formant or F1, the next boost we find will be F2 and so on.

Formants are very important for musical instruments as well. Have you ever played an acoustic guitar that sounds fantastic on some notes, with ring and sustain, and then dull and flat on others, with the note dying quickly? That's because the body of the acoustic guitar is missing formants to boost certain notes and harmonics.

Our Formants

What does this have to do with singing? Your voice relies on formants to do something basic yet remarkable – human speech. Go ahead and say the common English vowels on a straight pitch: A-E-I-O-U. Your vocal cords produced the same sound waves, yet our ears will have heard very distinct, separate vowel sounds. How is that?

It is because as you changed the position of your tongue, lips, jaw and larynx (that bump in your neck that goes up and down as you swallow) you changed the size and shape of your mouth and throat. Since your mouth and throat are your main resonators, just like acoustic rooms, and you changed the size and shape of them, well then you changed the value of the formants.

Our EQ System

The formants act like much like an EQ on a stereo or mixing board, they filter the information from the sound waves (harmonics) to make not only vowels, but to color the sound, brighter, darker etc. The interaction of the formants and harmonics have a profound effect on your ability to hit notes strong yet relaxed, or to have a complete vocal flameout.

If the formants align to the harmonics properly, they will boost parts of the sound wave in such a way that energy is sent back to the cords, assisting them in the work of holding back air and the muscular balance for pitch. If the formants align in a less than optimal way, you will often experience cracking, straining or worse.

When It Goes Bad

One of the biggest problems singers experience is the first formant not wanting to let go as the dominant resonating force. Basically, in our lower, speaking register (often called "chest voice"), we are getting a primary boost from the lowest formant. We feel this boost primarily in the throat, and the sympathetic vibrations also cause the chest to resonate, hence the term "chest voice."

The problem is, this first formant (F1) doesn't like to let go. In fact dragging F1 up as high as we can is how we yell, and since it is a basic survival mechanism, we are all good at yelling.

As the singer ascends to the top of the chest register – the nervous system will usually kick in a go to a yelling posture. This will manifest itself with the chin raising up, the mouth going over-wide, and the tendons and muscles of the neck bulging. This almost always sounds terrible, and worse, can damage the voice from the strain. How do we stop this from happening?

Hooray for Vowels

The most efficient way to control formants is through vowels. Thinking about making tiny adjustments of our resonators, or trying to force the larynx down can become artificial sounding and a bit too much work.

The secret is to use vowel sounds that will encourage optimal formant/harmonic relationships – and that's what Jaime is doing here in *RYV*. All of the different sirens and vowel combinations in *RYV* are designed to make good, consistent formant and harmonic relationships that will enable the singer to increase range, volume and tone color choices.

When Jaime talks about the "core of resonance," he is actually guiding you into the common physical sensation of good formant/harmonic relationships. Instead of getting stuck in the lowest formant, you are being guided to allow higher formants to take over the main resonance job on your upper notes.

Just keep in mind that as you work through these exercises, there are acoustic reasons for everything you are doing. If done correctly, your resonators and sound waves will begin to experience a very happy friendship, and you will be able to truly Raise Your Voice!

John Henny is regarded as a true Teacher of Teachers. He has taught vocal technique to voice teachers all over the globe. As a writer, John served as vocal expert and columnist for Backstage Magazine, contributing articles on vocal technique and health. He also created the Science of Vocal Bridges lecture series as well as Voice Teacher Boot Camp, where John trains voice teachers on-line. John's students have starred in Broadway and touring productions of Jersey Boys. Miss Saigon, Godspell, Les Miz, Movin' Out, Avenue Q and more. John's students have had starring roles on Desperate Housewives, Hannah Montana, Camp Rock, Glee and have been finalists on American Idol and The X Factor. Students have been signed to Interscope, Warner Brothers, RCA and Universal, to name just a few. John maintains a private studio in Los Angeles where he provides vocal technique and rehabilitation to the entertainment community. His website is JohnHenny.com.

Need More Guidance?

Make sure to check out my website, jaimevendera.com, for new products and updates. Follow my blog at jaimevendera.com.

Join the Vendera Vocal Academy at VenderaVocalAcademy.com to unlock your true singing potential. Vendera Vocal Academy has HUNDREDS of instructional videos, mp3s, and PDF guides, as well as online group lessons and student discounts for products and private lessons as part of tuition! If you still want some one-on-one guidance, click on the LESSONS link on my website and follow through to my online teaching page to book a lesson and fill out the Vocal Assessment. I'll get back to you ASAP to answer some of your Vocal Assessment questions pre-lesson to see how you are doing.

No matter where you live in the world, I can help. Feel free to book a Skype lesson or contact me at Jaime@jaimevendera.com to book an in-person session. I've taught online via Skype for years now, and it works nearly as well as an in-person session. All you need is a high-speed connection to your computer, a webcam, and a set of headphones.

My setup consists of an Alesis keyboard and mixer, Editors Keys SL150 USB microphone, a Blue Eyeball webcam, a pair of TC Helicon monitors, and G-Recorder Pro, which is an app that works with Skype to record the lesson, which I send to all my students. The SL150 by Editors Keys is a condenser mic specifically created to be directly input into your computer via USB and is a great tool to have for online lessons as well as recording. I always have a set of headphones in  case my student is listening through monitors as well. The latency of Skype tends to echo my voice on the other end when using the TC monitors. As long as we can see and hear each other, we're in business. I also have a portable setup consisting of an iPad with Skype app and an iRig KEYS Pro keyboard plugged into my iPhone to run the iGrand piano app. When I travel, I use an iPad mini for Skype on Google Hangout and my TUNED XD app on my iPhone for my exercises. Any similar setup will work for you.

Well, enough jabbering for one book. Again, this is my life passion, and I truly hope I have inspired and helped you to proceed to the next step along your vocal path. Good luck and God bless. C-ya next book.

God Bless,

Jaime Vendera

Acknowledgments

I want to personally thank all the people involved in bringing this book together. Thanks to Daniel Middleton for turning the interiors of every one of my books into a work of art, as well as believing in me enough to co-partner on 711 Press with me based on one simple vision of turning TV shows and movies into book form, Molly Burnside for another fantastic cover and years of support, Kevin Hoops for another set of amazing pictures, Benoit Guerville for more superb illustrations, and my typo checking/idea inputting team of Faisal Sheikh and Doug Skene for double-checking all my literary mistakes, Austin Jenkins for mixing my audio files , and my amazing editor, Richard Dalglish, for keeping 711 Press and Vendera Publishing in check.

Thanks to several of my friends for helping me along the way, including Tommie Armstrong, Emi Jo Hammond, Abby Hunter, and Kirk Gilbert for bringing Sing Out Loud alive, Brian Kelly for making Extreme Scream 1 & 2 so much fun to record, James and Rocco Gillette for being the coolest students on the planet, Jim Gillette, Tony Harnell, Myles Kennedy, James Labrie, and Sahaj Ticotin for believing in what I teach and spreading the word, the Vendera band, Keith Gilbert, Tim Odle, and Scott Stith, for without you, this music would not exist.

A special thanks to several of my partners, including Sean Daniel for bringing the *Beyond the Voice* video series to life, Shawn Fields for FINALLY making screaminglessons.com a reality, ha-ha, and Ken Ludden for creating TUNED XD, finally making my *Digital Vocal Coach* idea more than just a dream stuck inside my head.

A super special thanks to my guest article writers, Matt Adams, Dallan Beck, Ben Carroll, John Henny, Dr. Timothy Jameson, David Aaron Katz, Anne Loader McGee, Eli Prinsen, and Lonnie Winters. Without your input, this book wouldn't be a complete work of art. Thank you for supporting me. To the Vendera Publishing authors, including David, Anne, and Dr. J, whom I've just mentioned, as well as James Lugo, Ray West, Liz Sabine, Valerie Bastien, Robin Gillette, John Henny, and many more to come. You make publishing a wonderful experience.

To my wife, Diana Vendera for supporting my continually creative ideas that are enough to drive any sane person nuts.

And a final thanks to my Lord and Savior, Jesus Christ. Without you, I am nothing.

Jaime Vendera is the author of a variety books and one of the most sought-after vocal coaches on the planet. Using the methods that he created, Jaime turned his two-octave range into six octaves with massive decibels of raw vocal power that enabled him to set a world record, shattering glass with his voice. When singers need more vocal range, power, and projection, or need to build up vocal stamina to perform every night, they call Jaime Vendera. Jaime states that "none of this would have been possible without God."

Ben Thomas of Dweezil Zappa says that Jaime is the "Mr. Miyagi" of vocal coaches, while Mat Devine of Kill Hannah considers him more of a "Yoda." James LaBrie of Dream Theater said, "Because of my lessons with Jaime, my voice is feeling and sounding better than it has in twenty years. I am spot-on every night. He is the Vocal Guru." Myles Kennedy of Alter Bridge said, "One time during a tour, I was so sick I could barely make it through the set. It looked as if we were going to have to cancel the next show. Jaime spent some time giving me some tips that helped me regain my voice. By the next night, I was able to perform the show. He is fantastic! *Raise Your Voice Second Edition* is THE book for singers. I recommend his books and his private instruction to ALL singers." Jaime can be contacted at jaimevendera.com.

CPSIA information can be obtained at www.ICGtesting.com
Printed in the USA
BVOW04s1431040215

386383BV00033B/745/P